James E. Hobbs is a retired gemologist, graduating from the Gemological Institute of America in 1976. Jim started his career learning the watch, clock and jewelry business in Woodsville, NH. He later worked in Baltimore, New Jersey, Pennsylvania and Sarasota Florida where he retired. His writing career has covered many years. His work includes over 300 books about various areas of interest including designing a 13 week adult course in Gemology, 25 childrens books that were read to over 850,000 children in 93 countries, history oriented photo books of various towns in New England, life experience books, humor and now after finishing his first mystery … "Jason Downer and Dee Dee investigations!

Jim can be reached at info@wmtn.biz

Most of the more memorable buildings in Woodsville were long before my time. I moved here from North Haverhill in 1941/42 with my grandmother, Grandfather, Mother and brother. As most old-timers know;Ted Hobbs was the Chief of Police here until his passing in 1955.

He attended every basketball game Ozzie and I played in. He even, somehow, found it necessary to attend to police business in surrounding towns, like Lisbon, Twin Mountain, Haverhill and as long as he was there he might just as well stop in to see how the game was going!

I remember one game in Twin Mountain. The dressing room was divided by a curtain. Spider Hubbard, myself, and others were making fun of their gookie center. Little did we know they were right on the other side of the curtain!

I played center and seldom even tried to out jump the monsters I was lined up against! I kinda thought it was going to be a tough game when the other center rubbed his elbow and said this is going to be fun ... crushing you!

Bob Dumais was our coach and early in the season he decided I was going to be a point guard when we had the ball because I was fast; and I was to play the center position when the opposing team had the ball.

The first trouble, after a pretty rough center jump ball, was when I moved out of the bucket to guard a forward that was charging through center court. I put my left hand out to guard him and, accidently, drove my thumb into his glasses! It really was an accident, unlike some of the other things I did later in the game.

Luckily the boy didn't get any glass in his eye and the game continued. I was hearing a lot of smack talk from the giant center. So, I had to use my head instead of my lack of strength! I would, during normal play, always keep a hand on the opposing center, just to let him know I was nearby. I altered the play-plan a bit, just for the giant.

I'd get up really close behind him and give his shorts a little tug. The more it bother him the more I did it. One time I grabbed his shorts with both hands saying "Down we go!" He turned around and was ready to fight. And, I was fully prepared to run!

My grandfather was standing outside, by the bus door as we left the stadium, the Twin Mountain team grouped behind him, glaring. The folding bus doors closed and I could see a slight grin on Pa's face!

Times were better in Woodsville back then. We had seven grocery stores, several barbers, Bagonzi's Restaurant, the Bowling Alley, the Orpheum theater and an 'A and P' store!

The first wood framed building on the west side of the tracks was the Weeks block. It expanded several time through the years, but, I am sure, in the beginning it was nothing more than a wood-framed, two story house!

Following is my rendition of what I believe it looked like in its earliest days........

Weeks first store was down by the covered bridge over the Ammonoosuc river, where we all learned how to swim and dive off the dam on one side of the bridge and from the center stone section in the middle of the bridge that protruded out a bit from the bridge, making a nice place to dive from.

However, the water wasn't very deep there and we hit the bottom more than once! We, of course, were diving from the upper side of the bridge!

Notice the sluiceway for moving logs down-river, lessening the chance of log jams! Not far from here is where the Ammonoosuc river ends and joins the Connecticut river!

The earlier picture of what I think the Weeks store originally looked like, was on the corner of what is now Central and Pleasant streets, between the present two banks.

The Weeks building left us with a tremendous amount of history and local lure.    One special character I remember was Shortie Millette. He lived in one of the apartments that were in a later built addition of the Weeks block, up Pleasant street!

In our kitchen was an oil cook stove. It was old and very heavy and there was an oil container off to the side of it, on a stand. My job, after the evening meal, was to take the can down cellar to where the big oil tanks were located, to fill the can. My hands smelled like kerosine most of the time!

On the other side of the stove was the hot water tank. It was about six feet tall and was always full of hot water! The stove had about four burners. There were round plates about six inches in diameter over each burner. If you used a special handle you could lift the cover over the burner. There was, always, a large tea kettle on the back of the stove and it too was always full of hot water!

Below were the burners. They were round circles of wicking that would soak up the kerosene as needed. Shortie Millette would come twice a year to clean out the groves the wicks sat in and instal new wicking! Shortie was part of our life!

As was Sonny McDonald. The doors were never locked and Sonny would dash in, grab whatever cloths needed to be laundered and hang the delivered items in the bar over the entryway between our hall and dining room.

There was a small sliding wooden panel between our kitchen and the dining room. There was a mirror in it on the dining room side. Its purpose was to slide food into the dining room and the dishes back into the kitchen. It was always closed.

We never needed it. The food was carried into the dining room! I always new when Norris Cotton was coming because my grandmother would set an extra place.

As kids we were in awe of Mr. Cotton. He was like a very different kind of person. He seemed interested in us!

He was soft spoken and talked to us like we were grown ups. Ozzie was starting to play baseball and Mr. Cotton talked to him like he was sincerely interested. Not the way most people are with kids. They ask questions the kids know damned well, by their tone, they aren't really interested!

Mr. Cotton seemed sincerely interested. He was not the normal lying politician like we have today! He and my grandfather were close friends. All of the local politicians would try to cosy up to Pa. But they never had a plate set for them, like Mr. Cotton did!

Mr. Sherman Adams was another of Pa's friends. He was a descendent of both John Adams and John Quincy Adams! He served as President Eisenhower's chief of staff for six years. Many years later when I was working in Laconia, Mr. Adams walked into the store to chat with the owner, Jack Sawyer. Jack introduced me to Mr. Adams.

Mr. Adams paused a moment, stared directly into my eyes a moment and then said, "You aren't, by any chance, Ted Hobbs' grandson are you? We then heard several minutes of "Ted Hobbs" stories! All good and very complementary of Pa!

My grandfather died in 1955 and I still have people tell me stories, good stories, about Ted Hobbs! Most of them are about when he took them home, put them in bed, pointing a huge finger at them; telling them to stay there until they sober up!

Those were better days. Mellower days. Friendlier days! Drug free days. Pre rent assist days! Pre food stamp days! Pre get your lazy ass to work days!

Anyway ... Back to the Weeks store, the first store on the west side of the tracks, an area that was covered with virgin white pine trees! Can you even start to visualize what this side of the tracks looked like with only one lonely building and a zillion trees?

Weeks soon put up a residence where Woodsville Guaranty Bank's back parking lot is now located!

## The Weeks family home, later home of E. B. Mann!

That is, likely, Luvia Mann on the front lawn, by the fence! The house was built for Mr. Weeks and his family.

The new Weeks store was built in 1860-61. His first store was in what is now known as the Legion Home, and he was in business in that building from 1859. Starting a business in the only building on this side of the tracks was most courageous!

But, business was brisk right from the git-go so he expanded the building along the side that would later be named Pleasant street, starting in 1889!

There were hitching posts in front of the Weeks store; something that continued as buildings along the street started to be built! In 1884 the Weeks block was sold to three local businessmen!

They were William K. Wallace, a jeweler, E. B. Mann, a pharmacist, and Charles G. Smith, a lawyer! They owned the block until 1893 when it was sold to Q. A. Scott, who was a forward thinking businessman. He expanded the size along Pleasant street as well as the width on the original store!

Mrs. Batties had a business on the second floor and suffered a partition fire in 1897! The damage was contained and there wasn't much loss for Mrs. Batties!

Plate glass show windows were installed in the front of the building in 1897! Four years later, in 1903, the block was purchased by Charles Hosford. He did some cosmetic improvements and resold the building in 1911 to Rudolph Stahl!

Mr. Stahl did many cosmetic improvements, most of them internal before selling to Herman Thompson in 1923. It was called the Thompson Block until 1943!

At that time, 1943, a couple of years after we moved to Woodsville, the store was sold to the Castello family!

It would take an entire book to list everyone that inhabited the confines of the Castello block!

This new part on Pleasant street had space for four small shops. The front was divided into four stores. There were several small spaces around the back of the Pleasant street shops; by the Henderson Hotel. These spaces housed Beatties Taxi Service, Nash Woodsville Company, and a place for Peter Tegu's Popcorn Machine!

When looking at the front of the building; the last store on the right end of the Weeks block was a jewelry store. It was owned and operated by William Wallace. He ran the business from 1875 until 1889!

Wallace was a horse lover and later cared for them on Wallace Hill the turn off on the left on route 10 just passed Walker Motors. It is now called Hastings Hill, because in 1920 it was bought by Perry Hastings. Carroll Hastings, the son, later ran the dairy farm and delivered milk in Woodsville and surrounding towns.

Frank K. Kittredge was next to operate a jewelry store in that same location. Frank was from Danville, Vermont.

Mr. Kittredge installed electric lights in his store in 1891! Mr. Kittredge was a horse lover, like Mr. Wallace before him! He, at one time owned five horses!

The next owner at that location, also a jeweler and optometrist, was Mr. R. E. Boemig.

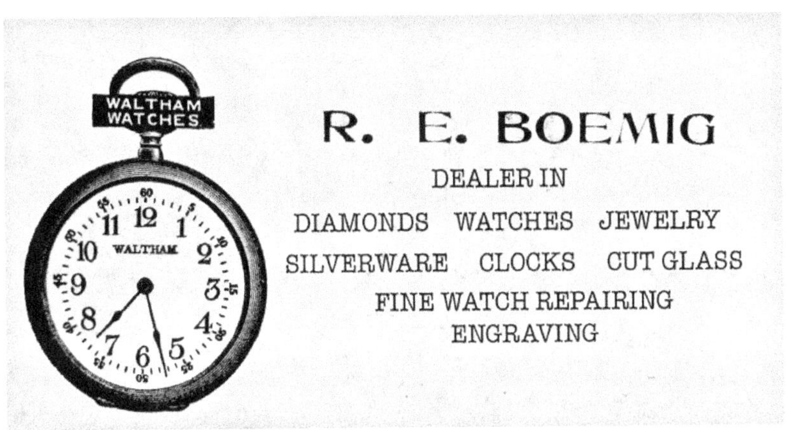


Mr. Kittredge, remained in business. although not in jewelry, around the corner in the Odd Fellows Block.

Here Mr. Kittridge sold sleighs, robes, and the remaining inventory from his jewelry store. He also acted as a pawn broker!

Mr. Boemig had previously worked in the Waltham Watch factory. Waltham, Mass.

Mr. Boemig served this town for 40 years! In 1912, the next building, The Parker House, caught fire and Mr. Boemig had to remove most everything from his store! Mr. Boemig passed away in 1938.

The next occupants of this space in the Weeks Building were Harley Kaiser and Frederick Mayo. They operated K & M Dry Cleaners and was located here from 1938 to 1942. Mark Burnham was a tenant here in 1946.

My family moved from North Haverhill to Woodsville in 1941-42, but I do not remember any of these stores! But, I do remember the next tenant which was Mrs. McMeekin! Florence  ran a dress shop here in 1953 and Ernest Welch, Jr, ran a gun and watch repair shop here from 1952 until 1957 when he moved his shop to Wells River, Vermont and then to Lebanon, New Hampshire!

Wilfred Larty moved the office of his oil company here until the Weeks Block burned in 1961. Mr. Larty then relocated to Holly street, off Ammonoosuc Street. Wilfred J. Larty was the elected Chief of Police until the early 40's when we moved to Woodsville. Wilfred asked Pa to run for the office and he did. But, at that time one had to live in Woodsville in order to be eligible to run for that office!

Florence McMeekin was next to rent this shop. Her husband was an engineer on the railroad and was in the legislature. She later moved her dress shop into their home on Chapel street, formerly the Dow home. It is about to be destroyed by the town!

Mr. Dows son was the first student to graduate from Woodsville high school, and went on to Dartmouth. The select board never found the nerve, and or, interest, in trying to preserve this house before it totally fell apart!

Back to the second shop from the right in the Weeks block ... a ladies garment store operating under the name of Howe and Gordon was one of the first businesses at that location, starting business in 1890!

They stayed at that location until the Fall of 1891, when they relocated into the new Opera Block! A shooting range was at this location for a short while. But, the noise and the idea of guns being shot between the two adjoining stores, was not acceptable!, so they moved up Pleasant street into the Music Hall, next to the Odd Fellows Block!

At this location, in 1891, Gasper Police opened the first fruit store in the village. He ran the business for a short while before Mrs. Batties moved her dress store here. She then, in 1891, for some unknown reason, decided to move the store back upstairs to her former location! That was in 1897.

The next enterprise to operate at this location was Charles Vergani. He opened a fruit market at this location in 1905. Gasper Police came back into his former location and was there for 5-6 years.

Charles Vergani then took the space to operate his fruit and confectionery store, from 1905 to 1914. His brother-in-law came to work for him. His name was Charles Christopher and in 1914 Charles became the new owner of the store! He operated the store for the next 33 years selling fruit, periodicals, cigars and candy.

We lived directly across from the Court House and the Christophers were our neighbors n So. Court St. toward Clay hill. Our neighbors toward Main street, the Field family, were also merchants in the Weeks block!

In 1938 Mr. Christopher added a soda fountain, a juke box, and a luncheonette in the back part of the store! Mr. Christopher sold out his business in 1947 to Charles Wood, more commonly known as Bunny! He later became the Register of Deeds in the left front office in the Court House!

The next store in the Weeks Block was occupied by Mr. E. B. Miller. It was located between the Christopher store and Weeks store on the pleasant street corner. Mr. Miller was earlier in business down on North Court street, below the underpass!

Mr. Miller was there until March of 1905, when in failing health, he sold his store to Bert U. Wells! By 1907 Mr. Wells moved on and became a travelling salesman!

In 1907 Frank M. Astle and William Delaney purchased this store from Mr. Miller. This partnership lasted only two years. Likely, the business wasn't great enough to support both of the partners and Wm. Delaney went back to his former employment at Armours Meat Co. at 38 Railroad street, where he had previously worked as bookkeeper and cashier!

Armour & Company had been doing business in Woodsville since 1905, dealing in wholesale meats! They erected a new building for their business in 1914!

Many worked at Armours, both in the plant and in the delivery of meat to stores. Many locals we employed at Armours, both in the plant and out delivering meat to stores!

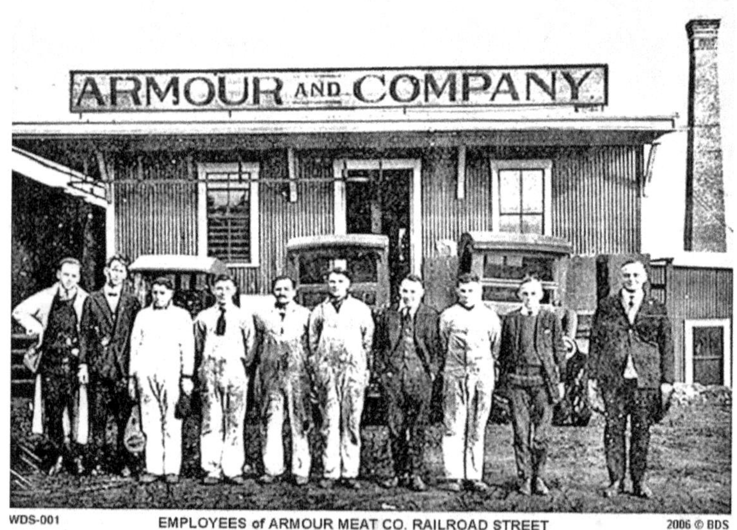


WDS-001     EMPLOYEES of ARMOUR MEAT CO. RAILROAD STREET     2006 © BDS
WOODSVILLE, NH CIRCA 1935

Armours closed this facility in 1972. Landy Veal took over The building from 1989 until 1993!

Our neighbor on South Court street: Marshall Field worked for Mr. Astle for seven years before purchasing the store in 1916. He stayed with the business for 32 years! He was an honest merchant and a wonderful neighbor.

Unfortunately, in later years, he suffered from Dementia! I remember one time when Mrs. Field came over, seeing me in the yard, asking if I would look for Billy. She said he had wandered off and was very worried.

This had happened a couple of times previously, so I was prepared to help. He was never very far away. He walked very slowly! So I hopped onto my pike and headed up School street, past the Library and out to Central  street, which, at that time was called Main street!

Once there I looked to the left toward downtown and then to the right where I spotted Mr. Field poking along, slowly, one small step at a time, looking downward, neither knowing or caring where he was headed.

I slowly road my bike up beside him and walked it along at his slow speed, for a short way. I then stopped saying, "I have to go home, Mr. Field. Will you walk back with me?"

He would face me, gazing at me for a moment and then, very slowly, would turn and start walking home. Mrs. Field was most thankful to see him safe and thanked me!

My grandmother made me a cold drink of Ginger Ale and grape juice, with a spoonful of sugar in it to make it fuzz-up, as a treat!

Mr. Field had sold the store to Leon Ward back in 1948. There was a back door to that store where bulk items were stored. Lee Tegu and I would use that as one of our short cuts to his fathers theater, the Orpheum! The back door was usually open. There were various products stored in barrels in the back room. Some, of which, I didn't recognize. But, something that surely wouldn't happen today, was dry cereal stored right beside a barrel of kerosine!

The new owner, Mr. Ward, passed away in 1952. It was vacant for several years until the fire in the Odd Fellows Block in 1955. That event placed Woodsville Furniture without a store space, so they rented the vacant store, until moving down the street, just before Woodsville Cafe.

Woodsville Cafe is now McAllister Jewelers, one of the longest running family owned businesses in Woodsville!

The first tenants in Weeks building, on the corner of Main and Pleasant streets, was Quincy A. Scott, who, with his brother-in-law, Albert Leighton purchasing the building and started a clothing and dry goods store, in 1875!

The business was called Scott and Leighton until 1889 when Leighton sold out and it became the business of Q. A. Scott. Mr. Scott sold the business to Isaac Stern in 1899.

Isaac Stern was from Island Pond, Vermont and operated the store as the New York Store! In 1908, after Mr. Stern died, the store was sold to Rudolph Stahl, from Berlin, NH, who operated the store for men's clothing!

Mr. Stahl owned the block from 1911 until 1923! He sold the business in 1920, to the Leibowitz Brothers.

Levi Kugelman was a well respected and longtime businessman in Woodsville. He was the first tenant in the new building next door to the Weeks block ... the Henderson hotel. Mr. Henderson had this hotel built after the Parker House burned in 1912.

Note the advertisement for the café next door.......

RAILROAD MEN ...... Remember you can get
a good quick lunch at the .......
## WHITE HOUSE CAFE
any time, night or day!
W. G. Mitchell, Prop

Woodsville, NH

Kugelman's had previously been in the Weeks Block, in a smaller shop on the Pleasant street annex of the building. That was from 1911 until 1914!

In later years the Kugelman store, operated by Bob Kugelman, was positioned further along the street where the "Shadow Box Art & Framing" shop is now located!

The elder Mr. Kugelman passed away in 1933. Mrs. Rosa Kugelman and son Robert, moved the store to 83 Central street in 1938!

My personal memory of the corner store in the Weeks block was the A&P Store. We used to collect discarded bottles which we returned for the deposit!  We got about a buck for a couple dozen bottles! But a buck is a buck back then as it is today!

A&P STORE, CIRCA 1940

The Atlantic and Pacific store moved here from the Henderson building in 1938. They broke out partitions up Pleasant street, allowing room for their new "self service" grocery store!

In January of 1961, the A&P Store moved down the street into a newly constructed building where the Bailey Buick Garage was located for many years!

Woodsville Motors became Bailey's Buick Garage, operated by C. L. Bailey and son Arthur. Mr. Bailey was, in earlier times a blacksmith in Woodsville!

## C. L. BAILEY
### =:= The Village Blacksmith =:=

General Jobbing and Repairing
Horse Shoeing a Specialty : : :
Satisfaction guaranteed on all work

### WOODSVILLE, N. H

Up Pleasant street, but still in the Weeks block, at #3 Pleasant street is where the Kugelman store was first located. Once they left in 1914 the space was taken over by Davis and Clough. They sold harnesses and carriages. They had purchased the business from Newton Lang.

Robert Large, an insurance agent, rented this space in 1936 for his office. He was representing the R. T. Bartlett Insurance Agency. Mr. Large moved the agency to North Haverhill, into his home, in 1943.

This space, the first up Pleasant street was taken over by the A&P; the interior walls were removed, making more space for the A&P!

There was still rental space up Pleasant street , in the Weeks Block. It was listed as being #5 Pleasant street! There was a cobbler at this location in 1885. His name was P. T. Browne. He was followed by the post office from 1886 until 1894 when it moved into the Opera Block! I believe it was the middle space in the Opera Block, between Scruggs Hardware and the side stairway to the Opera House. Which is the space where I opened my first street level store, called Jim's Curios.

I repaired watches, and sold phonograph records, paint by numbers, candles, jewelry and gifts! It was a short lived business, after which I moved to Baltimore!

It is believed Mr. H. Willey was selling pianos at #5 in 1895. He was only there a few months before moving into the Sargent block.

In 1916 W. Howard Forbes opened a music store and was selling pianos and player pianos! He also sold Edison phonographs and records. He also sold an automobile, or two, on the side. Mr. Forbes died in a car accident in 1918. His business was sold to Dodge and Garner to become a branch store for their Bailey's Music Rooms! That store was located in the Mulliken Block in 1911 and was destroyed by fire in 1916! This block will be discussed later in this book!

Back to #5 Pleasant street, the annex of the Weeks block. This was the town and police office in 1929. Sheriff Arthur Davis and deputy Roscoe Rinehart were the officers on duty!

When we moved from North Haverhill we bought our house from Rinehart! Davis and Rinehart also operated a taxi service out behind the Odd Fellows Block!

From 1935 until 1955 #5 Pleasant street was occupied by the Wander In Gift Shop! The shop started upstairs by Lora Watchie, a telephone operator I believe, in the Odd Fellows Block. It was run by several people. This was likely some sort of  cooperative shop, like todays consignment shops!

It was moved downstairs around 1938 and they were selling discarded library books! The shop, soon after, was sold to Harold Miller and Weldon DeCoteaux. After the war the shop was moved up the street to the Mulliken block, where Woodsville Book Store later rented! The Wander Inn later moved to Main street in Lisbon NH!

In the last part of the Pleasant street annex, at #7, by 1886, the business there was L. E. Collins bottling business!

The above pictured box and bottle labeled "Collins" Woodsville, NH, were given to me by Dana Leonard, from Glencliff, New Hampshire, and Swainboro Antiques, located in Rumney, NH!

It is rumored that Mr. Collins may have bottled other than soda pop, from time to time, and in 1901 was appointed as the liquor Inspector, for some strange reason!

In 1915, the Collins space was taken over by a barber by the name of Gilman Blake. Blake was a well known barber and was still in the barber business in 1935!

Kinne and Paddleford operated a business of some kind, possibly an ice business, somewhere in the basement of the Weeks block! This was in 1885-1886.

Most of the small businesses along the Pleasant street annex were taken over as business increased in the A&P. The spaces were needed for the ever expanding A&P business with space needed in the rear of the block to accommodate the Atlantic and Pacific delivery trucks!

There was a stairway installed between the A&P and the second store allowing a front entrance to the upper floor of the Weeks block. There were quite a few businesses on the second floor, including Judge Castello's office and court room!

I am familiar with his court room as I visited there once. It wasn't a murder case, or a burglary. It wasn't for any crime that hurt anyone. I wasn't an escaped convict!

But, as I learned at a very young age ... having a car repossessed isn't the end of a problem. It is the beginning!

It seems the car is sold at sheriffs sale and the victim, me in this case, has to pay the amount of the loss!

I was allowed to borrow from a credit union and spent the next year, or so, paying it off! It is similar to paying for the hay and grain for a horse you do not own!

In the meantime, of course, I had purchased another car! Hell you can't take out a date in a wheel barrow!

Some of the other people upstairs in the Weeks block, actually the Castello block by that time... were; Mrs. E. J. Batties, a milliner, was there in 1879, and longer. Marion Donnahue, a hair dresser was there from 1929 to 1956. Dr. Prickett, Dr. Blake and Dr. Baker were the dentists upstairs!

W. E. West, a photographer, Mrs. E. G. Mason a dressmaker, Ernest Gobeille a tailor, W. S. Pitt cleaning and pressing, Frank Lorenzo a shoemaker, Mrs. Murray Clement with a toilet shop, and my barber Felix Roy who was up there until 1956 and had a little problem when his towels that were hanging over a heater to dry; caught on fire!

Two years later as Parker Spooner was rebuilding the empty A&P spaces for a new Aubuchon Hardware ... fire broke out again. This time the entire structure was destroyed!

Others who were burned out were Mike Castello's Woodsville 5 and 10, Mitchell's Luncheonette, Larty Fuel, Law offices of Castello and Bruckner!

Later, in 1978, the Lafayette Bank was erected on the old Weeks/Castello lot. Other banks replaced it ... Indian Head Bank, Fleet Bank, and the Laconia Savings Bank, which is now the Bank of New Hampshire!

I am sure I left out many things that should have been included in the history of the Weeks Block! Things like Shorty Chase that waited outside the area, waiting for people coming out of the theater, just in case someone needed a cab!

After seeing the present condition of Woodsville's downtown district; it is hard to believe we had three taxi's!

We don't even have an Uber! The previous "NOW" picture is depressing to say the least! And even more depressing after seeing what it was like, not too long ago!

What went wrong?
Who is at fault!
Who will fix it?
Until those questions are answered I'll move along to another major Woodsville Building, just up Pleasant street from the Weeks Block ... the Odd Fellows Block! There have been two! The first wasn't very significant! It was just a small residential building near the far end of Pleasant street!

In 1882 the Tabor Block, a three story residence, saloon, at the western end of Pleasant street, was purchased by the Moosehillock Odd Fellows Lodge!

The lodge hired Dalton & Bray to do the remodeling; turning the building into a meeting lodge!  Water was installed in 1886 after the aqueduct system was installed in Woodsville! The ground floor was divided into three stores!

In 1882 St. Luke's Episcopal Church started a library of sorts here. Then, in 1883 a printing office opened and in 1885 one of the ground floor spaces was occupied by a hairdresser, a Mrs. M. V. Mahurin from Haverhill Corner! She left after a short period of time.

Another business occupant was a Mr. S. E. Nutting who operated a home furnishings store here in 1883 to 1886.

Ai Willoughby moved his meat market from the basement of the Weeks block here in 1886. He later, in 1889, sold the business to Truman Glover, who moved it to his own building at 83 Central street!

A cobbler open a business on the second floor in 1886. His name was C. G. Browne. He moved from the small police office in the Weeks Block!

T. H. Aulis was a barber here in 1890! And, in one of the apartments a dressmaker, Mrs. L. C. George was located!

New furniture arrived for the Odd Fellows hall in time for their 76th anniversary celebration in 1895. It turned into a large celebration with a ball in the IOOF Music Hall, next door!

The Music Hall was a large and ornate building built by the Odd Fellows in 1890. It was located between the Odd Fellows building and the Weeks block. There were stores on the street level, including a shooting gallery! A. H. Vallee operated a restaurant here until about 1893 when he sold out to Charles W. Johnson from Wells River.

There were many happenings within this building, including musical performances by the Lyceum Theater Company and by the Mackay's Boston Comic Opera Company.

Photographs of these two buildings are hard to find, even in my collection of over 3000 local photos!

Tragedy struck on May 15th, 1901 and both the Odd Fellows block and the Music Hall were completely destroyed!

However, 100 years later, a program was found when a door casing was removed in a house on Smith street. The owners brought it to me. The edges were singed and pages were very fragile, but I was able to scan most of the pictures. The booklet advertised a musical group that would be soon visiting the music hall. The fire was tremendous and burned items were forced into the air, landing in a large area of town. This booklet must have travelled all the way to Smith street,before landing! Or, perhaps, someone picked it up in the pile of rubble that was left on site. Either way, these people evidently used it to shure up a door frame!

# FISK JUBILEE SINGERS

**The Music Hall and IOOF Buildings burned on May 15th, 1901**

## THE SECOND ODD FELLOWS BLOCK

**11-17 Pleasant street,was built by James R. Lowe, a local contractor and building mover, was completed in 1904!**

It was a large three story building, covering the entire area of both of the former I.O.O.F buildings, and a large part of Pleasant street!

The building opened in 1904 and the Woodsville Furniture Co. occupied all, or most of, the street level floor! They carried Furniture, Carpets, Rugs, Mattings, Lace and Musslin Draperies, Portiers and Window Shades!

Jerry Abbott and Dennis Rouhan operated the furniture store. Mr. Rouhan bought out any partners in 1911. He hired a Mr. Charles Adams as an undertaker in 1917 and purchased his first automobile hearse the same year.

The hearse, prior to then, was drawn by a pair of black horses! One died and Mr. Rouhan replaced it with another black one! He, also, used the horses for pulling the furniture wagon in later years!

Herbert Swan became a partner in the business and lived in Haverhil Corner. Paul Ricker, after graduating from the American School of Embalming in 1946, also joined the firm!

By 1948 the furniture store had expanded; taking over the entire street level space in the Odd Fellows Block!

The small building showing on the back right side was H. O. Taylor's Garage! Before taking over the first floor; the middle store was rented by James McLean and used as a pool Hall. That was in 1904.

The tenant, at that time, on the far right, was run by F. K. Kittredge selling carriages and buggies!

Woodsville Post Office occupied space in the Odd Fellows building in the middle ground floor space from 1904 until their new building was completed on South Court street in 1942.

The Selective Service Office moved into the Odd Fellows Block in September of 1943. When they moved out the furniture store took over that space.

Six offices on the second floor in the front of the building, overlooking Pleasant street, were taken by the New England Telephone Company that moved here from Wells River.

The amount of cables and wiring that was needed drew daily crowds watching the operation! That was in 1904.

The telephone 'central' was installed here in 1909 for White Mountain Telephone and Telegraph Company!

Other offices on the "telephone" floor were, Attorney R. U. Smith, Woodsville Printing Co., F. P. Dearth Insurance, A. D. Davis deputy sheriff, Grafton County Farm Bureau, Attorney Fred Wright, Judge H. K. Davison, Miss O. J. Baird milliner, Henry Emerson barber, Mrs. K. J. Baird's Temple of Fashion, and the Selectmen's office, were all here in 1916!

The rear portion of the second floor and all of the top floor were occupied by the Moosilauke Lodge, I.O.O.F. The top floor was, also, used for social events, dances, etc.

The American Legion occupied some space on the third floor until they moved into their present location at the end of North Court street!

There were some small buildings behind the Odd Fellows block as follows; in 1887 A. E. Davis had a livery stable for the Parker House. In 1893 Dr. W. H. Hornblower had a veterinary office for the care of horses and cattle. Unfortunately, the good doctor died only a few months after opening the office! Another veterinary, Dr. Nichols took over the practice, moved away after only a few months!

Davis and Rinehart had space in this same area for use as a livery stable. That was in 1917. They rented horses and rigs. By 1917 they converted to a taxi service!

My little friend, Thelma Douglas, told me of the time her mother and a visiting aunt rented a team. I wonder if it was from  Davis and Rinehart?

Anyway, the ladies were crossing on the lower level of the double decker bridge, between Woodsville and Wells River, when a train roared over the top, cinders flying on the ladies and their horses below!

Is this what you expect after paying a toll?

Anyway ... The horses bolted and threw the ladies into snow banks off to the side! The horses and the passenger-less wagon were recovered by the Opera Block, a short while later, and the ladies were shaken, but unharmed!

**The Double Decker Bridge**

**The Toll House on the New Hampshire side!**

There was a small ice house for the Wentworth Hotel, somewhere between the Odd Fellows block and the hotel.

Forest Chase had a garage off the back side of the block, as did H. O. Taylor....

The following picture was taken from an early motion picture from the thirties. The entire movie can be viewed by clicking the bottom right IOOF link on the front page of ... www.whitemountainbiz.com

The small portion of a building showing on the right side of the following pic is the last store, #5 Pleasant street of the Week's Block!

The Odd Fellows Block burned to the ground on January 13th, 1954. We watched the flames, over the post office, from our front porch at 34 So. Court street!

The loss of this large building put many businesses out in the winters cold. Some of the businesses were moved into the Court House by the post office. Dearth Insurance Agency and Farm Bureau was businesses that moved there.

Soil Conservation moved to the federal building! The Grange and Goodwill moved their meetings to St. Lukes Parish house at 121 Central street.

The Parish House was completed in May of 1914. Many had utilized the Parish House, including band concerts on the front porch and Grange meetings.

Woodsville Progressive Club also met there. The basement is where the kitchen and dining room are located.

Before we stroll back down Pleasant street I should mention the loss of Dr. Dearborn's house and office, at 19 Pleasant street in the Odd Fellows Block fire.

Doctor Dearborn purchase the house beside the Elementary school, formerly owned by Dr. E. M. Miller.

As we turn to the right on Central street and stroll by the town park, with the large shade tree and park benches, we reach a dirt road leading to a gravel parking lot behind the park!

One summer evening my grandfather decided to walk home for supper, instead of driving the ole 50 Hudson! As Pa approached the gravel road a car appeared from the parking lot, stopped to enter Main street and blocked Pa from crossing.

There were cars on Main street keeping the car from entering the street. Pa just stood there, standing tall, with his badge, uniform, and gun, (which I still have), visible.

Suddenly, the driver of the car jumped out and put his hands up! Come to find out, the man was one of the ten most wanted and thought he had been caught by the Chief of Police in Woodsville, New Hampshire. Good job Gramp! Even if you weren't looking to make an arrest! Pa got written up in Detective Magazine for that arrest!

In the gravel parking lot, in earlier times was the Mann residence! The house was built back when Mr. Weeks put up his store. It was to have been his family residence! It later became the home of the E. B. Mann family.

After the house was taken down, and the gravel parking lot made, and the ten most wanted removed; the lot became a favorite place for movie goers to park their cars!

Once the movie came to the end, they could exit the theater through the outside door in the back of the theater to the left of the stage!

After leaving the theater through the back door, they could walk passed the back wall of the Wander Inn Shop, and cross Pleasant street ... to their car!

But that could only be accomplished after the Mann house was taken down! Obviously!

It appeared to be a grand house, with a large barn to the left rear side, just beyond Scruggs Hardware's back door in the Opera Block. In fact there used to be a cellar hole there at one time. Hmmm! Doesn't seem as though there would be a cellar under a barn! Barns were, usually, just on stones!

There was a stone wall in increasing heights; starting at the street and continuing to Dr. Millers vegetable garden in back of his house. I guess the cellar hole could have been for the house, but by the picture it doesn't seem right. But, I know of no other building at that location!

As I am thinking about moving to the Opera Block; my mind drifted to buildings in town that had a rail siding! I could only think of three, you know of more?

**The first two that come to mind are right in line on Railroad street ... they are Holbrook Grocery Company .....**

**and Armour Meat Company!**

The engine from the lower yards would bring the Armour car in back of the Holbrook car; drive up to the depot and then back the two cars down the side rail to Railroad street.

It would back to the Armour building, drop off the car ... pull back toward the depot and drop off the Holbrook car, or cars and take the engine back to the depot and return to the lower yards just south of the "Dry Bridge"! You do remember the dry bridge, don't you?

If you walked half way across the Dry Bridge and looked down over the fence, you would see the lower yards, where empty freight cars were organized.

The dropped off cars would be left by Armours and Holbrook Grocers for a day, or two, before picking them up by the engine and taken back to the transfer station!

Are you wondering where the other siding is?

It had been pretty-much forgotten until the snack bar was being removed by Woodsville Pizza. The siding tracks were caught by a pay loader. This siding went from the main tracks, between the Pizza shop and Trendy Times, toward Smith street where the oil storage tanks once stood.

The rail siding went to the backdoor in the lowest level of the Red Mill, where supplies would come by rail and be off-loaded from the side rails!

There were, likely, more, but have leaked from my memory! I guess one could call the turntable at the first engine house, leading into the repair stalls, could be called side rails! I'll include the roundhouse turntable, just in case! I call it my, Ooooops! picture.

In 1907 our original roundhouse caught fire. What started the fire I do not know. But, the above picture of an engine in the turntable has a bit of a story behind it.

It seems an alert mechanic working in the roundhouse sheds noticed the fire and tried to do something to save whatever  he could. I guess an engine was a good choice!

He evidently jumped into an engine, started it and attempted to save as many as possible, one at a time! It was a most heroic thought, but, unfortunately, he didn't check to see if the rails on the turntable were aimed in the right direction and drove the first engine into the base of the turntable. This, naturally, put a holt on saving more of the engines. There were several in the roundhouse sheds at the time.

The young man's idea was certainly a good one, and had the result been better he would have been a hero!  I believe most of the engines, in time, were salvaged!

I am strolling down Main street heading toward the Opera Block. I was a tenant there twice. The first time I was in an adjoining room suite I shared with my good friend "Bud" Chase. I was doing watch and clock repairs and Bud was doing taxes for individuals and businesses. The door between us was always open, unless income tax agents were in town. I'd shut the door then!

We would go down to Jesse Brown's "Town Shop" by the theater entrance, for coffee everyday. Paul Tetreault would usually join us and we would likely dream up a way for him to pay! Jesse Brown, a daughter of the building owner, Mr. Henderson, was a nice lady, a very prim and proper lady!

I was in the Town Shop one evening having a cup of coffee. No one else was there and we started talking about this, that, and something else. Her watch came up in conversation. She had a Hamilton. This is way before the battery watch days!

She told me she had too much electricity in her body and her watch never ran more than a month after picking it up from the repair shop! I told her if she stopped the watch because of electricity, she would have been electrocuted years ago! We laughed. Jesse had a good sense of humor, and asked me to explain. I said I didn't really have an explanation, other than it wasn't electricity stopping her watch.

I asked if I could work on the watch. I wouldn't charge her a cent until she says it has run longer than ever before, after being repaired! Jesse said ... "Deal" snapped the watch off her wrist and handed it to me!

By then I was in a street level store beside Scruggs Hardware, in the Opera Block. I took her watch completely apart and cleaned it thoroughly! I then laid the parts out on white tissue paper and inspected each and every piece. I found nothing wrong. I waited until the next day and did another inspection, this time with a stronger eye piece! I still found nothing.

I checked every tooth in every wheel. I was determined to find something so insignificant that it wouldn't have been seen during a simple cleaning!

I didn't find even a slightly bent tooth in any of the gears! I ran it through a demagnetizer, just for the hell of it! Nothing! Now, I have had contact with a lot of electrifying ladies in my life. Even married a couple. But, none of them electrocuted me! Some wanted to, but never did!

The parts just sat there on the white watch tissue. It is a special tissue that doesn't have any lint in it. It is just for watchmakers. The only piece I hadn't checked was the pallet fork. This is the part that changes rotary motion, like gears moving, into lateral motion which is a side to side motion, like letting the gears to move one second at a time! You'll be repairing watches by the time I get through with this!

Following is a pallet fork. it moves side to side letting off one tooth at a time from it's closest wheel, the escape wheel! One tooth, one tick, od tock ... whichever!

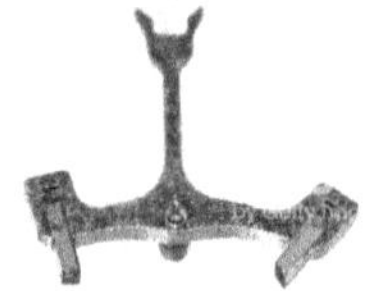

The two teeth on the pallet fork are jewels held in by a tiny drop of shellac! After cleaning a watch the repairer places a tiny drop of oil on each of the pallet jewels, to reduce any wear on the escape wheel! For some unknown reason I flipped the pallet fork over with tweezers, and looked at the underside closely! Yup! There it was! A slight chip on the edge of one of the pallet jewels. I loosened the shellac holding it, replaced it with a new one, cleaned the parts again, just for the hellovit!

I reassembled the watch, polished the case, timed it out for a few days and then returned it to Jesse!

I left after a free cup of coffee, saying I'll be back in a couple of months for payment, if the watch is still running. We laughed and I moved to Baltimore soon after!

About six months went by before we were able to come back on vacation. I stopped in to the Towne Shop for a couple of coffee. I asked if her watch was still running. She smiled and said, how much do I owe you?

I said she didn't owe me a cent. I felt like I was a Governor granting a stay on her electrocution! We laughed and I got another free cup of coffee!

The thought of covering the Opera Block is eating at me. I'd much rather make up stuff to write about, than to have to do research. I took a lot of the information in this from my dear friend Katharine Blaisdell, and from Whitchers book on the history of Haverhill, and from personal experiences living in Woodsville, 75 of my last 81 years! I spent the first six years in North Haverhill!

I've thought of a way to delay writing about the Opera Block. I'll do a short bit about the watering trough! The first picture is when the stone trough had a wooden enclosure around it.

The above pictured water tub was installed around the time the Opera Block was built, in 1890! Whether the wooden enclosed tub was built at that time, or not, I do not know. It may have been a bit earlier!

The next picture, when the through was moved more toward the center of the Opera Block, makes me think the tub may have been built before the Opera Block was. There were horse and buggies long before the Opera Block was built?

The above picture, with no clock in the tower, and the water trough moved more in front of the Opera Block instead of it's location in the previous picture! This one should date about 1915, because of no clock and the date of the vehicle!

In the previous picture the tub appears to be further away from the Opera Block than in the earlier pic! The one below is a winter pic?

This winter scene looking down South Court street and the water tub that appears to be turned a quarter turn from the previous picture.

The picture on the next page is an interesting one.

It is of the water tub with interesting wagons gathered to water the horses. (a gathering place!)

The building would be the Express Building and the pic is before the depot was built!

The bicyclist is in front of the Opera Block, if indeed, it had been built at this time!

There is no underpass under the tracks to North Court street. There is what is quite apparent to be a "Dry Crossing" over the tracks just passed the trough and no depot!

I guess it is time for me to research the Opera Block, and get it over with!

About the only personal thing I can add is the fact that, while working at McAllister's Jewelry ... I worked on the tower clock, long before it became electrified! The remains are embalmed in the Montshire Museum in Norwich, Vt. Another stupid move those responsible have made!

The word is the town wants to create a museum. In my mind they have already made a mummy out of Woodsville's downtown district! All that is left to do is to embalm it! Which, I am sure they will do!

I'm really putting off writing about the Opera Block. It is going to be a long and tiring journey!

So, I'll tell you about the latest audition for an episode on Saturday Night Live. Actually, it was the last meeting of the Haverhill Heritage Commission. I attended as an honorary member. It was the most unusual election I have ever witnessed!

It looked like the chairman and secretary were acting out an Abbott and Costello skit, preparing for a gig on Saturday Night Live! One person nominated the other. Then 'other' seconded the first other. Then there was a vote taken! They voted for themselves and one of them won! Don't ask which one. It might have been Costello!

There were three people there that, up until that evening, displayed a desire to join the heritage. All were longtime Haverhill residents, or from families long established in the community. I know I was not wanted at the meeting, the chairman, or unofficial chairman, has declared in no uncertain terms his feelings ... even going to the point of making outrageous implications, that had absolutely nothing to back them up. Kids would be scolded for continually lying!

Two of the three applicants gave statements indicating they were no longer interested in joining. The third asked if the chairman wanted him to join. He was told he did not, because of his obvious bias when it comes to Powder House Hill, or as it is now being called ... Powder Puff Hill!

Yet, the chairman is obviously bias, himself, toward these applicants, all of which are outstanding residents, but do not have the same priorities as the chairman! Who is calling the kettle black? Some people have been swore in very shortly after their request, but these folks have waited months!

This is certainly discrimination, don't you think! I've suggested a multi million dollar class action law suit is in order! When the minutes, if they are not lost as they may have been about the last election, ... I'll get it in this book somewhere. I'll guaranty it won't be anything like I have just written and I have about 10 witnessed to the actual event, against only two for Abbott and Costello! Who will you believe?

It doesn't really matter, because the minutes will likely come up among the missing!

**********************

That does it. I cannot put it off any longer! I'll go to my bit about the Opera Block! Bare with me because this is going to be extensive!

If you look at the block on the South Court street side you will see where some of the second floor is higher than the rest. This is because of the height of the stage in the actual Opera House, and the raised tier of seats for patrons.

**There was a room directly under the seats where many of the school pictures were taken!**

The Opera House was managed by Mr. E. B. Mann. At one time it was the center for local entertainment. There were dances, plays, and acts by travelling professional entertainers.

The hall was decorated in a most elegant way and the high ceiling gave the acoustics an amplification making one feel they were actually participating!

The plays were applauded whether you were sitting in the front row, or in the balcony seats!  The Opera House held 600 people! In 1893 the play "The Country Fair" packed 900 people in! I wonder where the fire Marshal was that evening?

The first movie in the Opera House was shown in 1901 and "Birth of a Nation" was shown in 1915!

The room under the slanted floor of the seats above, was used to hold dances and many class pictures were taken there! In 1905 two firemen had to be posted during every performance!

There were double doors as entrance to the theater on the back part of the second floor. Space on that floor not being used by the theater was split up into office spaces.

There was a stair well on the main floor between Mann's Drug Store and the two other retailers on the South Court street side.

After climbing up a few steps there was a landing. Up more stairs took you right to the double door entrance to the theater. There were stairs out in front of the building between the drugstore and the banks that went straight up to the middle of the offices on the second floor.

This is where Bud Chase and I had adjoining rooms. There was a hallway between my space and the front of the building where a hallway lead to a room directly under the town clock. This is where the "Town Fathers" met!

Things were different back then. Anyone could walk into a meeting, whenever the fathers were there, and sit down at the table! And,you could join in the conversation. Believe it or not ... they would even listen to your ideas, and/or problems!

In the earliest days, like in 1891, Blake's Barber shop was one of the busiest spaces on that floor! He was in the front of the building right over the bank!

He later moved his barber shop into the Weeks block. But, he kept one chair in the original space!

In 1893 a Mr. F. M. Valdes, opened a tailor shop on this floor. He later moved his business down to the bottom of Clay Hill, on the river side, by the entrance {today} to the community field! His wife became very helpful in continuing his business! Mr. Valdes later fought as an American in the Spanish American War!

After returning from the war; Mr. Valdes reopened his business and, also, started an organization of American veterans of the Spanish-American War!

In 1894 the law offices of Smith and Sloan were renting office space in this location. Five years later their partnership dissolved.

Mr. Sloan continued the business in that same location on the second floor of the Opera Block, while Edgar Smith, with his son, Raymond, moved up the street to the Mulliken block which will be discussed in other pages in this book!

Other lawyers opened offices here at later times, including Charles Hosford in 1900 til 1919. Fred Wright also opened an office here, as did Francis Edes at the same time Bud and I were there! Attorney Zellers opened an office here in 1941.

In 1898, Mrs. Eliza J. Batties opened her millinery business over the bank in a front corner space overlooking Main street! She had, previously, operated her business in the Weeks Block back in 1879!

Mrs. Batties' daughter Miss L. Maude Batties also opened a millinery shop here and ran it from 1895 until 1926! One year before she closed her business she married a Mr. Carlton.

Helen Aldrich, from North Haverhill, was working for Maude Batties in 1913, as was Mrs. Hazel McDonald, from around 1908, or before!

Gray's Beauty Shop also operated here on the second floor of the Opera Block, from the late 1920's until 1938. The owner of the shop was Miss Mabel Noel. Miss Noel sold the shop in 1938 to Priscilla Layton.

The floor was the home to many dental offices during the ensuing years. They included, in 1916, Dr. Perley Speed, who had been located in the Mulliken block until the fire.

Charlie Christopher's son Leo, also had an office here before moving to Maine! Dr. F. G. Weeks also maintained a dental office here!

Deputy Sheriff Arthur Davis also had an office on this the second floor of the Opera Block! He occupied the small room under the town clock, from 1897 until 1930.

This was the same room I mentioned was there by Bud Chase's and my offices; the town fathers office!

From 1917 until 1922 the H. P. Hood milk company had a branch office somewhere on this floor. The office manager was B. A. Blossom.

Cummings Construction also had offices here in 1929, as did Winthrop Klark, the photographer. That was in 1948. He later purchased the Lovejoy building, presently the Antique Rose, as his photographic studio.

This building later became the home of Sipprelle Studio, where a great many school pictures were made!

The Welfare office was here occupying space on both the second and third floors until 1972, when it moved to the Henderson Block!

Offices for the White Mountains Regional Assoc. offices were here until 1972, when it, also, moved into the Henderson block! Ashley Hazeltine was the Executive Secretary from 1938 until 1952. She was followed by David Cassedy who maintained the office until it was moved was moved to Lancaster, New Hampshire, in 1959!

The new Henderson Block seemed to be a popular place to move to! It was like a smiling child on Main street in Woodsville!

The Railroad Men's Clubroom, in November of the year 1895, five years after the building was completed, moved into the third floor of the Opera Block! The Knights of Pythias also moved here for a short while. They soon moved into the top floor of the Tilton block, after finding out they could not sublet any of their space to others!

In 1898 the top floor of the Opera Block was finished off. The John L. Woods Club, a social club for young men living in Woodsville, moved in and opened a reception parlor, gym, music room, and other rooms. In the year 1900, Ward and Douglas' law office opened on the third floor as did a tailor, Mr. H. Charland!

Fire struck the Odd Fellows Block on Pleasant street in 1901 making many businesses in need of space. This made the Odd Fellows homeless!

As a cure they were able to lease space in the Railroad Men's Club. They maintained that lease from 1914 until 1938! Opera Block Apartments purchased the Opera Block and began restorations in apartments in October of 1979!

Some of the well known renters of the street level of the Opera Block, in more recent years, were Scruggs Hardware, McAllister Jewelers, and Americas longest running family owned drug store ... E. B. Mann & Company!

Just to the right of the main street entrance was a door to the banks. There were two teller windows in the bank. I have marked the entrances with X's! Note no clock in tower!

The doors on the front entrance was for the two banks!  Once inside you would see two teller windows, side by side. One for the Woodsville Guaranty Savings Bank, and the other for the Woodsville Loan & Banking Company!

There was a brick structure in the basement that was a support for the vault. It had the appearance of an arched bridge. I recently photographed the old jail in the Court House and found several of the identical structures there. There were several vaults in the Court House, for securing important papers and documents!

These structures were, obviously, made by the same person! I noticed the one in the Opera Block basement by accident. The height wasn't as high as needed for a person wearing a western hat. I was constantly bumping my head!

Scott Moody, another member of the Haverhill Heritage Commission, at the time, was with me, inspecting the building. Scott was a bit shorter and didn't have that same problem. The lighting wasn't that good at that point, but, upon closer inspection we could clearly see it was a structural support for a very specific purpose. It finally dawned on me, having been a renter in the block back in the early 1960's; that the location was right under where the bank, banks!, had been located!

We were inspecting the building for the Heritage Commission, back then it was doing things that mattered, and not being run (ruined) as it is today, under a nearly totalitarian manner ... by limiting new members that might have a different view as to the future of the commission, which presently appears to be doomed!

You can email me if you agree the present dictator of the Select Board should be replaced, either by impeachment, or by ballot!     info@wmtn.biz

***********************

Back to the banks on the street level of the Opera Block! The Woodsville Loan and Banking Company started in a room in the freight station in 1890. It later changed into the Woodsville National Bank!

If you had business to attend to you would merely finish at one window then step to the side to the other window, and/or other bank!

Horace (Hod) Knight was treasurer of the Savings bank in 1914. He was. also the cashier! He became president of the National Bank ... 1938-1959! Henry Keyes, the founder of the bank, then became chairman of the Board!

H. Scott (Scottie) Mitchell worked for, and was a trustee of, the Savings Bank for 42 years. The Mitchells lived on Oak hill and Mrs. Mitchell, Nina, was the librarian.

I used to clean the basement of the library, and do other chores, for the library back in the forties. Nina Mitchell gave me free piano lessons for my chores! Mrs. Mitchell was the librarian from 1941 to 1964! The school swings were by the north

side of the library

The Woodsville Free Library was established in 1894. Charles B. Drake, a  druggist, was the first Librarian! Ira Whitcher built and donated the present library!

Let's get back to the bank, located on the right side of the Opera Block, on the Main (Central street) side! Mrs. Mildred Heath worked at the banks for 55 years, from 1918 until retirement in 1973! Guess I'd better finish up with the bank ...

The follow pic is of the original bank interior!

On that corner, and side, of the block, in 1917, a 12 foot extension was added, extending toward the street! The next pic shows the extension. Notice the alarm on the top of it!

This picture was taken during a 4th of July parade! The building to the right was the Weeks/Mann residence!

The banks moved into the new bank facilities in 1956.

In the front space, left by the bank, in October of 1961, one of Woodsville's most respected men, from one of the most respected families in Woodsville, moved into the empty space and opened his law office...Mr. H. K. Davison! He was a lawyer, member of congress and a gentleman!

An entire book could be, and should be, and may well be written, by me, about **H. K. Davison!** Although thinking about book number 108 is a bit premature!

This space was later the home of the Dearth Agency, Marjorie McBride, agent. The insurance business was sold in 1975 to **H. J. Graham!** Or, better known as "Jack" Graham, a Woodsville High School sportsman/graduate!

Jack is #4, beside Bob Smith #4, Guy Kelley #11 and John Bagonzi #5. And, of course, Nick Pendo!

I'll be doing more Woodsville High sports pice on the last pages of this book!

On the South Court street side of the opera Block were two store spaces. Let's talk about the one on the corner toward the Post Office!

The first occupant on this side of the block was the store of G. E. Lane! That was in 1891. His clothing business got off to a grand star due to his ingenious advertising on the side of a circus elephant that was coming to town at about that same time. The animals in the circus came by train and paraded down South Court street, passing his store, heading toward the Community field.

I have a circus elephant story. I have told it before, so if you've all ready heard it; just skip along a page, or two, and miss something, because I never tell the same story twice!

Anyway! We, as you well know by now lived at 34 South Court street, right across from the old Court House. We sold the house to a wonderful couple and it pleasures me each time I drive by, knowing their children grew up, right where I grew up! And the family has as much pride in the house as we did! After my grandfather died; I had plans to open a watch repair shop in one half of the garage. But earning $1.00 an hour kinda ruined those plans!

But I still have memories! ... The circus came to town by train and the animals were unloaded and taken to the Community Field in colorful wagons by way of Connecticut street. But, after the circus closed up they returned to the depot on our street, So. Court, and right by our house!

I still remember how excited we were when we saw the first elephant head appear as it trod up Clay Hill! Once they got to our house, one of the elephants, and its attendant with a stick, stopped! It stopped right in front of our porch where we were standing!

It not only stopped, but turned his enormous head to look directly at us! Then the darned thing started walking toward us, between the two trees on our front lawn.

It walked right up to the railing on our front porch. My God! It had enormous eyes, and they stared directly at us! It's truck touching the railing on our porch!

If you look real close ... closer ... even closer, you will see me!  You didn't, really, look close, did you? My God, you are gullible! If you believed that you will certainly believe the rest of this story! I may just fill it with some stupid stuff!

Naw! I can't do that! Anyway, the elephant just stood there, looking at us; the attendant poking it with his stick, the elephant completely ignoring the little jabbering jerk!

The monster slowly turned his head and strolled back to the street, between our two front trees! The attendant hurried along behind thinking the elephant was under his complete control. I've got news for you little guy; he's the leader and you are the follower!  And stop poking my new friend with that stick! That is the last I saw of either one! I miss the elephant!

The advertising created by G. E. Lane had a good start, however the business began petering off shortly after the circus left. Mr. Lane soon closed and moved his business to Lancaster. Next here was Mr. F. P. Pray, also a clothier.

In October of 1893, he too moved, but not to Lancaster! Mr. Prey moved downtown to former Sargent store! It is, at the present time, empty! The most famous businesses in that building was Mr. Sargent!

The original store!

The Woodsville Post Office moved here from the Weeks block in 1894, In September of 1910, the post office moved to the Odd Fellows Block!

In November of 1910 a jewelry/clothier from Bradford, Vermont moved into to the vacant post office. Doe Brothers had been in the Mulliken block and the clothing part of the business stayed there!

In 1913, Doe Brothers jewelers sold out to another jeweler/watchmaker, C. Tabor Gates! Mr. Gates was active in the town as a member of the school board, and likely, other boards!

Mr. Gates moved to Lisbon to operate a store there and sold his local business in the Opera Block, in 1923 to Samuel McAllister!

Mr. Gates finally ended up in Littleton, where he had originally learned his trade!

Samuel McAllister, Sr. came to Woodsville in 1901. He was a fine watchmaker and, after coming here, worked for Doe Brothers and Mr. Gates. Samuel bought the business in 1923. Sam's grandson, David, moved here to take over the business in 1952. David later, in 1960, moved the store down the street by the Bowling Alley!

Scott McAllister, one of three children of David and Shirley McAllister, is now operating the jewelry business!

In the store front on the South Court street side, closest to the Post Office, was a general store of Howe & Gordon, who moved to this location from the Weeks Block and opened their store in September of 1891.

Katharine Blaisdell states the store sold everything from groceries to horse blankets! And we all know Kay was an excellent researcher!

In January of 1900, Howe and Gordon retired and sold out to Fred Mann and W. B. Cushman. Both of the new owners had been employees of the previous owners and knew their customers well!

Mr. Cushman soon retired and his shares went to Roscoe Olney! Roscoe had been an employee of the Brick Block at the Highland Street and Perkins Place railroad crossings.

Only six weeks after becoming a partner in the store; Mr. Olney, at the young age of only 28 years, died, from typhoid fever!

The Olney and Mann sign hanged over the front door for well over a year before it was finally taken down! A new sign was put in its place ... Mann & Mann, being operated by George Henry Mann and his son Fred Mann!

The Mann & Mann delivery wagon!

George Mann fell into the grain elevator in 1912, like his Brother Ezra did, and never fully recovered! Ezra fell in the elevator at E. B Mann drug store, however!

George and Fred were in the process of firming up plans to move their business into the new Rowden Block! Fred followed thru with the moving plans around July of 1913 and his father died the next month!

Ezra Mann bought out the remaining stock and with Joseph M. Howe as manager continued the business.

The last business to operate in this, the last street level store in the south end of the Opera Block was Scrugg's Hardware! This store ran the full width of the building with a back door and stairs to their share of the basement. The space also ran along the width of the next store!

The first tenant here was Howe and Gordon and the last store, before Scruggs was Mann's Opera Block Grocery!

Rhett Scruggs came to Woodsville from South Carolina in 1906. He first worked for Mulliken's Hardware Store in the Mulliken block.

In 1910 Mr. Scruggs and N. B. Perkins bought out the sheet metal and plumbing part of Mulliken's business. The couple set up business in the downstairs of the C. H. Davison's hall, which was the building of a replaced school that had been moved onto the Davison property.

Mr. Perkins sold his share of the business Mr. Scruggs. Rhett Scruggs moved the business to one of the first business blocks in Woodsville .. the "Brick Block", between the two railroad crossings.

Rhett Scruggs moved from the Brick Block to the Opera Block in 1922.

Mr. Scruggs died in 1940 and his nephew, Paul Scruggs, one of the nicest businessmen in town, took over the hardware store!

Scruggs hardware took good care of the plumbing problems in Woodsville and many surrounding villages! He had very able employees like Edgar Stanley, Eugene and Wilfred Lamarre.

Parker Spooner worked for Paul from 1972 to 1974 when he bought the business! He moved it to 147 Central in 1979 and was in the process of moving it into the corner space of the Weeks Block left by the A&P, and then the fire struck!

# Woodsville's Memorable Buildings

And now, the middle store on the South Court street side of the Opera Block, prize, goes to me, as I was one of the later people to rent the store. I'm more than a bit upset that my dear friend, whom I complimented earlier in the book; didn't include me in her fine book, Haverhill, New Hampshire in the Twentieth Century! By Katharine Blaisdell  2000!

I am sure she will forgive me, because she was a very forgiving person. She had a wonderful, and impish personality. I remember on one of my many late afternoon visits, after being on the road promoting the benefit of advertising on my small business web site ... www.whitemountainbiz.com!

Katharine was sitting in her chair, I immediately handed her a book and said, "Kay, I just completed an historical fiction!" She looked at the cover, set in on her lap and placed her right hand on its surface. I waited! She finally looked up and said, with a slight twinkle in her eye, "Isn't that what we all write!"

*"God Bless Katharine Blaisdell!"*

Anyway, one of the first renters of the space in the Opera Block between Scruggs Hardware and the side doorway to the stairs, was 'DRUM ROLL PLEASE' ............

As you can see by the previous Scruggs picture, McAllister's Jewelry store was in this location. I think Pearl Zuncore moved her beauty parlor there after they left, and then I opened there as "Jim's Curios"! I wasn't there long enough to have a picture taken! That was back around 1961-or 62!

Alfred Lamarre was the Chief of Police at that time. I remember a young man coming into my store saying the cop on the street suggested he come and talk to me.

He said his father was campaigning in Woodsville and he really needed a place to rest, undisturbed! I said he wouldn't be disturbed in my store because no one comes in! He laughed. It wasn't a joke! I was very serious!

Anyway, I said he could rest in my desk chair in a back room, just incase someone happened to wander in to ask directions to a real store!

The young man left, and returned in about twenty minutes. He had his father with him. He didn't have to introduce him, it was Barry Goldwater! I was really impressed. He was the first big namer I had ever met, on a one on one basis.

I later met movie stars, the vice president, famous football and base ball players, like Johnny Unitas … and played in a golf tournament, sharing a golf cart with Phil 'Scooter' Rizzuto! He was a real gentleman. He was interrupted so many times with people wanting his autograph, that he didn't get his golf shoes tied until we got to the first tee!

He was very patient with each autograph seeker and took his time writing a beautiful perfect signature! And, he always thanked *them* for asking him for his autograph. Wow! What a gentleman!

But, at this time, I was really impressed meeting Barry Goldwater. And, it saddened me that he didn't get to be president. I guess it was his answer about ending the Viet Nam war. He said he would bomb the hell out of them! It scared people, but I think perhaps he was right, but wasn't the kind of man that sugarcoats things!

I don't know, or care, who occupied that space after we moved to Baltimore. I was getting $8.00 to $10.00 to completely service a watch at that time. In Baltimore, I was on percentage. I received 30% of the retail price for the repair. That averaged, to me, about $25.00 per watch! About 300% increase!

How that all happened was this. I was sitting in Barry's chair, with my feet on the desk, just as Barry had done. I was reading a watch repair magazine and saw an ad for a watchmaker-manager wanted in a department store in Baltimore. I made a call and was in Baltimore a week later for an interview. A month later my store was closed and we became southerners!

The Martin L. King riots put a quick end to my wanting to stay in Baltimore! We picked up and moved to Phillipsburg, New Jersey!

I previously mentioned the Brick Block, while telling you about Rhett Scruggs. We might as well look that building over next! However. I just thought of a story my little friend, Thelma Douglas told me! I am sure it was a true story, because Thelma was sitting in a chair on her front porch when she told this to me. Her feet didn't reach the floor and they would move if she got excited! And, at one time, near the end of the story she put both hands over her eyes! You will know when that happened when you read the following story.

****** My mother, Mary Douglas, would walk to Woodsville, from our house in Wells River, (Later known as "Tilly's") every afternoon that my father, Jack Douglas, was working in the engine house in the far end of town.

She would sit on the stone wall on the upper corner of Main and So. Court streets, right across from Mann's Drug Store.

Mr. Mann had just moved into the new Opera Block building from his former store that was located in the building just below the wall she was sitting on!

A celebration was in progress. It was opening day for the Opera Block and for E. B. Mann's store! The celebration was in progress as the new building opened its doors.

Thelma said her mother was mesmerized by the number of people gathered there. She had never seen so many people in one place, before in her life!

My mother was enjoying the music and watching the crowds of people gathering around. Some of them were dancing and others were singing!

All of a sudden the music stopped, my mother heard drums roaring! Everyone suddenly turned to look toward the roof of the building!

**Mother gasped at the sight of an acrobat balanced on the top of the building..............**

I know of no actual pictures of this event, and, yes, I did a photoshop number on this pic!    So what!

### And now to the Mulliken Block!

The original Mulliken Block was built in 1900, by Adna F. Mulliken, as a hardware store. Mulliken had been in a partnership in a hardware store in Wells River, Vermont, since 1875.  He had, also, managed the Coosuck House in Wells River, in earlier days!

The actual construction of the Mulliken Block started in August of 1899! Lawyers Smith & Smith were the first to sign up for offices on the upper floor!

Doe Brothers, were jewelers and clothiers from Bradford, Vermont, and were the first to open with a street level store in the new Mulliken Block.

They were located on the far left end of the block in the earlier days, before the fire! They later moved to the right end, the annex, the part with four upper window!

This is the part of the building that is still remaining. I cannot help but think that was a lucky move!

Doe Bros. were about as diverse as I am in my present store, White Mountain Trader.

However, I do not carry overalls, stable blankets, along with Edison and Victor talking machines. But I did just purchase a few horse collars!

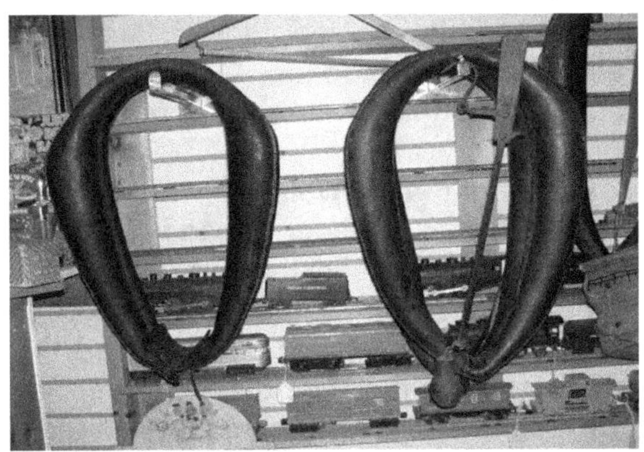

And, I just bought 2000 horse shoes. But, they are going fast so you'd better order now! Actually, they are about half gone. People are making lawn sculptures out of them!

Back to the Mulliken block. All that is left of the building, after the fire in 1901, is the annex part!

When I had Jim's Curios in the Opera Block, I did watch repairs for other stores. One of my accounts was Doe Brothers in Bradford, Vt.

Mr. Doe was not a watchmaker, but he was a cagey guy. Every once in awhile he would say, Mr. Hobbs, I had a terrible time adjusting the time on Mrs. So and so's watch. Please be a bit more careful in timing them out before you deliver them!

I knew damned well he wasn't regulating any watches! But, as I stated; he was a cagey cuss. He was just trying to let me know he was checking out my wok!

On one occasion Mr. Lynn Doe asked me if I would go to the basement with him. He wanted to use the space in a back room to display more merchandise. We went down and the room was full of clocks and other things. He asked if I would be interested in purchasing any, or all, of the items.

I said, yes, and offered him $1.00 for each item I handed out of the side window, where there was a slanted street, or driveway, right beside the window. I was driving a white Plymouth convertible I had purchased from Walker Motors in Woodsville, at that time.

I put the top down and loaded the car with as many clocks as I could fit in! I was whooping along on the flat below Wells River when I notice a flying missile in my rear view mirror.

It was a large shelf clock and it was spinning in the air. There were no cars behind me so I stepped on the gas and was entering Wells River before the clock hit the road!

The interesting thing about this is that there were two Edison talking machines packed in the car, likely leftover stock from the store! Not a bad deal at $1.00@!

A two story annex was added on the north end of the building in 1901. There were two store spaces on the street level and an apartment upstairs. When I was a lad, Mr. Gobielle, a tailor, and his family, lived in that apartment!

E. E. Craig grocery store moved into the Mulliken Block annex and was still there during the fire in 1906!

Mr. Craig, in 1909, sold his grocery business to the Richardson Brothers! Mr. Craig then went to work for the Armour Meat Company and soon became the manager of their Woodsville store!

The E. E. Craig delivery wagon!

Richardson Brothers only ran the grocery business here for a very short time. It then remained an empty space until 1911 when Mr. F. E. Cadwell leased it!

Mr. Cadwell, in 1915, sold the grocery business to a local man, Mr. Lynn Miller!

The main building, the part with eight windows, burned to the ground in 1916. What little material that remained was used to build the building where Walker Motors once operated their car dealership.

Immediately after the building was finished it was used to store things from the hardware store, like overstock, outdated merchandise, etc.

In later years it became a Ford dealership. That was in 1912 and was operated by H. C. Gale. The Bartlett-Mulligan Garage was here in 1914. They sold Ford, Cadillac and Overland automobiles! Mr. Wiggin was the mechanic and ended up owning the business in 1915! Wiggin moved away and in 1920 it became Central Garage!

In 1935 the garage was operated by J. Harvey Walker and Seth Eastman, who had moved from their location on North Court street, or "Haverhill Road" as it was called in earlier days! That building was just passed the Nash dealership owned by Silvio (Seavey) Pellegrini.

Prior to then there was no throughway from Chapel street to Central street. With the large part of the Mulliken block gone; there was now room, not only for a fire station, but an outlet for Chapel street!

At that time it became nearly impossible to purchase new cars during the war. So Walker and Eastman turned to selling grain and feeds, as an alternative to going out of business!

As soon as the war ended Mr. Eastman sold out his portion of the garage to J. Harvey Walker and the business continued until it was moved up on Route 10!

Auto parts stores came and went at this location for a number of years. The latest is Fisher Auto Parts and the employees there are very friendly and helpful!

William J. Walker, the father of T. Bordon Walker and J. Harvey Walker ran the tiny building alongside the Mulligan block, selling gasoline, in 1946!

The kind of gasoline sold changed from time to time. He was selling Amoco, as per the sign, when this picture was taken!

I think the square cement base for the Amoco sign is still there, right next to the old Mulligan annex! It has four threaded bolts, one in each corner, to secure the sign! If you take notice; you will see they all tip toward the Annex!

It appears to me that some hot rod driver, likely in the winter, ran into it. It appears the car may have been right up on the sign base. I imagine it would have been a 1938 Pontiac Silver Streak, with vacuum shift! Probably a coupe, silver color, with original large hubcaps!

Awe, dam-it-all, as you have likely guessed, it was me! I bought the car from J. Harvey Walker for $275.00! I only have three payments left and that baby is mine, all mine!

Anyway, I was friendly with Johnny Golden, at the time. He lived in Littleton. On this occasion; I drove to Littleton and we jaw-jagged for awhile. I then suggested we race to Woodsville, and I took off, tires a smokin'!

I reached the bottom of the hill entering Bath and couldn't see a single car behind me. I continued around the stone abutment for the bridge just south of Twin River Lodge, and headed toward Guilmette's flat. I looked in the rear view mirror and knew they would never catch me now, and eased off the gas as I flew under the train trestle on the flat!

There was no one in my rear view mirror as I approached the "Welcome to Woodsville" gateway!

I glide across the "Dry Bridge", skid around the corner at the end by the Fullerton Brothers Garage and head down Smith street.

I drove down Smith, turned right to Central where I turned left toward downtown. Still no cars in the rear view mirror! Back then, when coming toward town you were in Stoneville, until you crossed the Dry Bridge. Then you were officially in Woodsville!

This all happened in the middle of the winter, but there was very little snow on the road, so there was no problem driving in town, if you drove slowly, and carefully. Neither of which I did! If I gave it a bit more gas the rear end would sway back and forth. If I gave it a bit more gas the car would turn sideways in the street, which I did, and slid that way, nose toward the wooden fence along the tracks. I knew I could put it back whenever I wanted, so I enjoyed the ride.

At Kelley's store I decided to straighten it out. But, instead the car turned facing away from the tracks! By Dr. Eastman's house I cranked it back and started sliding sideways again, facing the tracks, And that is exactly the way I ended up teetering on that GD sign base!

The boys from Littleton pulled in a few minutes later and we popped a few caps! The Chief of Police after my grandfather died was Alfred Lamarre ... who came strolling by only minutes later.

There was gasoline, oil, and brake fluid pouring from my car onto the sidewalk! Alfred asked me what we were doing. I said we were having a couple of pops and would be gone in a few minutes. He continued up the street. That is back in the day when cops patrolled the streets! They'd likely get rolled if they did that today!

We jacked the car up until it was higher than the bolts and then pushed the car off the jack. We had to do that a couple of times before the car was prepared for take-off. I had enough gas to get me around the corner onto South Court street where I lived and, perhaps, enough brake fluid to stop me once I get there! That was about 60 years ago, so the statute of limitations must have run out by now!

Across the street from my store is the Highland street crossing. There is/was/still is a large building between the two crossings, Highland, spelled back when as Hiland, and an identical crossing at Perkins Place and Mill street!

Between the two crossings was a building where a railroad employee managed the controls for raising and lowering the gates! I doubt if it was a job where you came to work in the morning and someone relieved you for the evening shift when the long freight came down from the north!

Or, perhaps, a person was sent up from the engine house, having information there as to when trains would be arriving, and posted a person there at that time?

This is the earliest picture that I have showing the crossing gatehouse! It appears by the fancy roof to be very early. There are no exterior stairs, so there must be stairs, or a ladder inside, for the worker to access the controls.

I have a better picture of the gate house when it still had no exterior way to get to the control room.

The building in the previous picture is that of the Brick Block, the first commercial building in Woodsville. It is presently, and has been for some time, an apartment complex.

Most of the early landlords that owned the building after it changed from commercial to residential had concerns for the renters. Galand Locke, for one, built a structure where residents could have a cookout!

This picture answers a few questions ..

1) were there really trains coming thru Woodsville? Yes, Margaret, there were, as many as 75 a day at one point in time!

2) was there really a wood fence between the tracks and Main street? I have a better picture of the fence that I will, hopefully, remember to include later!

3) yes, there was an outer stairway to the gate tower!

And, the first commercial building in Woodsville was located between the two crossings!

There is a bunch of history in that building which I will try to relate. I do not remember a siding ever being there! I wonder how they unloaded merchandise for the various stores, and/or wholesalers! I guess the lower yard engine brought them up and took them back; between arriving trains!

I guess I just proved myself as an all-time fibber, because, there, right before your very eyes, is a siding between the gate tower and the building!

But, I did say, "I didn't *"remember"* ever seeing a siding there!" There are one hellova lot of things I do not remember. And, others that I am trying to forget!

My friend, Dana Leonard, an ex-railroad man was just in. I showed him the above picture and asked how they got the freight car there!

He thinks, and he may well be right, that the track the freight is sitting on, continues over the crossing, heading toward the depot. If you look closely you may agree!

That may well be true. If so that track probably followed toward the depot to a place just before the underpass crossing where it might have connected to the side rails that went to the Holbrook Grocery Company and to Armours!

After giving it some serious thought, and believe me at 81 my thoughts seem to float around in some unknown space. But, every once in awhile I am able to collect them and a vision fills the void that used to be my mind!

With that admission and having given time in getting the recall button to work, the fog is starting to lift, and I envision a side track following along side a fence on Railroad street. This side-rail would have serviced Merrimack Feed Store that must have received stock by train at one time or another.

The side rail would then continue toward the underpass and depot where it crossed the road at the corner of Railroad street and Oak hill!

## THE BRICK BLOCK

The Brick Block is listed as being at 2 Perkins Place and 42 Highland street. Back in earlier days Highland street was called Hiland street! I threw that bit of trivia in just because I wanted to!

This building was, sometimes called the "Brick Store"! Likely because some of the businesses did sell to consumers, but others were more like distributers!

The building was built in 1883 by Henry Ramsey! Mr. Ramsey, besides become a large landlord, was also the postmaster in Woodsville from 1863 until 1868!

Henry, we were on a first name basis, he called me Jimmy, was the local station master, too!

Walter Stickney and Frank Prey were the first to go into business in the Brick Block. They sold everything from storage barrels to ladies shoes!

The next to go into business here was Davison & Bailey and were there in 1886 when Seth Stickney purchased the building! Seth came to Woodsville in 1883 and for the next three years was in business downtown, with T. W. Stickney, in what was, up until recently Hovey's Shops and then Huberts!

**Stickney and Pray, prior to being in the Brick Block, was in the Hovey's spot way back even before the E. A. Sargent store days!**

A relative of Mr. Stickney gave me the following shoe button hook advertisement!

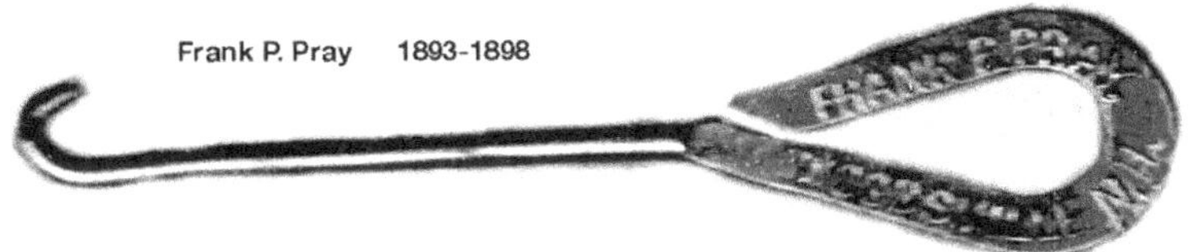


This Sargent picture was back when downtown stores were stick built, pitched roof, buildings! {houses!}

## Back to the "Brick Block"!

Stickney Brothers did a large business buying salt and flour by the railcar full! They also purchased large quantities of fresh produce from local growers!

They sold ice creepers and horse blankets as that was horse and buggy times! At a later time, the brothers sold out. That was in 1898 and the new owner was Charles Whitcher!

Whitcher took on John F. Page as a partner and the business operated as Page and Whitcher. It appears Mr. Page inserted enough funding to get his name first on the store marquee! However, shortly after; Mr. Page left and went back to his old job as a salesman for Cross Cracker Company!

Mr. Whitcher had a new sign made and continued along as the sole proprietor. In 1904, Mr. C. O. Whitcher sold out the inventory in his store and, subsequently, the building too!

The building was purchased by a group of local businessmen who had formed a company called, "Brick Store Company". The principals in the firm were: Mulliken, Wright, Hosford, and  Land & Webster!

The firm immediately started seeking a renter for the former Whitcher store!

Enter Cyrus Cameron, who opened a furniture store in the block!

Back in January of 1906 Butson's Market moved their business into the basement of the Brick Block! They had recently suffered a fire in their building on North Court street! They stayed in the Brick Block cellar until the Fall of 1907 when restoration of their own building was completed!

Mr. Cameron decided to move his furniture store down the street into Davison Hall, and in 1911 proceeded in doing just that, early in 1912!

Mr. Rhett Scruggs moved his plumbing business out of Davison Hall, into the Brick Block.

Around 1922 Mr. Scruggs moved, again. This time to the Opera Block, into the South Court street side, in the last space toward the post office! Mr. Scruggs kept storage and working space still in the Brick Block!

Mr. Leonard Dodge opened a restaurant in a newly decorated space in the Brick Block in 1913! The business was advertised as a restaurant and lodging house. I remember Mr. Dodge taking the shortcut from Central street to the post office using the cement steps my grandfather made in our backyard, on, what I believe was on the Fields property.

It was, like, a handshake deal! There was a wide cement wall built to divide the two properties and the steps were definitely built on the Fields side.

There was a huge butternut tree near the steps and our attic was lined with newspapers covered with butternuts drying. I remember handling the fresh butternuts and getting sticky hands that were practically impossible to wash, from handling them before they had dried!

The dried nuts were very hard to crack open! I had a favorite crack in the cement floor of our cellar and if I set the nut just right, it would break open with just a slight tap with a hammer!

I don't know why I keep interrupting with childhood memories, but I'm not going to hit the delete button! Rip out the damned page if it bothers you!

Back to the Brick Block .... In 1914 the syndicate sold the block to a Mr. John A. Colby.

In 1916 the entire basement was rented to the Woodsville Cheese Company! They produced a product called "Health Cheese"! The cheese company moved their factory to a facility near where Shaw's Market is presently located (2018)

In November of 1923, the plumber Rhett Scruggs, now relocated in the Opera Block, purchased the Brick Block! He redid the entire block into rental apartments.

By the year 1956, the block was owned by Seavey Pellegrini, and known as the Pellegrini block. Seavey owned the Nash Automobile dealership located beyond People's Market on North Court street, near the underpass!

Across the street from the Highland street railroad crossing was another early building ... the Variety Store!

This store is the building directly across from the Highland street crossing, on the corner of Central and Elm streets! It was built in 1899  by George Smith.

The Smith Store was a variety store selling everything from soup to nuts, kitchen supplies, cigars, graniteware coffee and candy!

Mr. Smiths daughter worked in other stores in town, but soon joined her father in his store. Business was brisk and they soon opened an ice cream business on the top floor!

In 1903 a lady named Lavernia Carpenter and her son came to Woodsville and purchased Mr. Smith's store a couple of years later.

The Carpenter family ran the store, known as the "Variety Store", for about twenty years. 'Vernia', as she was commonly called, sold the store in 1921, after expanded the front a couple of times! She soon moved away!

Her son, Henry Carpenter, was called back as requested by Mary Randall. Mary's late husband owned the coal business in town and Mary requested his help running the Coal Sheds on Mill street!

Mr. John Straw, a railroad man, was next to own this store. He purchased it in 1921! The Straw's continued using the Variety Store name until changing it to the IGA store in 1937.

Mr. Gould bought the store in 1944 and reverted the name back to "Woodsville Variety Store"! Ralph Pillsbury bought the store in 1948 and sold it to Wilson Lewis who ran it as Lewis's Red and White store from 1961 until 1961!

There have been various businesses here since then, including Riach's Red and White, John Fullerton's John's Sport Shop, Doug Olsen's Pleasure Products, Scruggs Hardware, and Bond Auto, before it became the infamous "White Mountain Trader"!

HEY! It's my book and I can advertise in it if I want to!

***************************

I think I'll take a stroll back downtown to South Court street where I grew up! Across the street is the Whitcher house, the old Court House, the post office, and way back when, the B&M Railroad Department YMCA!

# Woodsville's Memorable Buildings

The B&M Railroad Department YMCA building, on South Court street, was located beside and just north of the court house, where the post office is now located.

The building was built by Ira Whitcher in the early 1800's. In later years it was the home of Ezra B. Mann, who leased it to the YMCA in 1900, nearly a hundred years later! A front piazza and deck was added in 1901.

In September of 1900 the YMCA opened its door to a membership of over 150 members! There was an anti-room between the main building and the barn, that squired a beautiful weather vane!

The YMCA soon became a home away from home for railroad men!  Within a month they were having classes ranging from mechanical drawing, telegraphy, penmanship and general math! They even had their own church! Within a year the membership grew to over 250 members!

Early in 1901 an emergency room was set up and well equipped to care for railroad men injured at work! Later, in 1903 the original Cottage Hospital was created and the injured railroad workers were sent there to be cared for!

The building was sold to N. H. Nutter in 1913. He intended to use it as his family residence. At that time some of the railroad men rented a room in the Opera Block and organized a men's club! About that same time there was a bowling alley on the second floor, over the banks! I doubt if that lasted long!

In 1916 the house was sold the Dr. F. E. Spear as a residence and as a place to practice medicine! Dr. Spear was Joanie Spear Kelso's grandfather!

The building was sold in 1940 for the purpose of building a new post office. Bill Brill was hired to tear down and remove the old buildings!

Mr. Brill was known for doing this and he would save as much of the structures as possible and used much of it when building new structures!

The new post office was up and running shortly after Bill Brill had the lot cleaned up!

A while back I mentioned the Cottage Hospital. so we might just as well go there now!  Around 1903, Rev. William A. Loyne, a Methodist minister, had developed a fond admiration for the railroad workers, and had been receiving contributions from time to time, for the purpose of building or leasing, a building to facilitate the growing need for a hospital!

The entire project was started with the donation of one dollar toward the cost of the building.

Back then when Route 10 was called Haverhill Road and coming from North Haverhill, passed dark hollow, the road dipped to the left toward what is now South Court street, where Tegu's Meadows Drive-in was located.

This was a stage coach road, at that time, and the road only went as far as Melody Lane.

Just before the turn, on the river side, was a building. It was originally called the Stage Coach Inn, Cobleigh Stand and then Cobleigh Tavern!

I am told, and I am sure it is so, that there were many a rough time at Cobleigh Tavern. There were lumbermen, railroad men, and men on the loose from who knows where! Plus there were the occasional late-in-the-day stage coach arrivals, that might join in the activities.

I am quite sure the environment was much like, in later years, in the Wentworth Hotel! In fact, I could tell you a few tales about the Wentworth … but I won't! No! Don't pester me. I took an oath in front of the old mounted Moose head that hung on the hotel entrance side, that I would never reveal any thing I saw or heard in that fine establishment!

Let's get back to the Cobleigh Tavern before I start telling all, or even some.......

The tavern was built in 1827 as the home for Dr. Angier, about the only doctor in town at that time. Unfortunately in 1836, the good doctor was thrown from his buggy and died!

Windsor Cobleigh owned the property in 1838. He turned the Angier house into a tavern and ran it for the next 25 years! From 1861 on it became a residence, and sometimes a boarding house.

Around 1904 the widow of John L. Davis, for the sum of $2500.00, signed the deed over to the Cottage Hospital!

Reverend Loyne, after obtaining the lease, started to renovate the tavern. It was a struggle, but in September of 1903, before over 300 people, the hospital was dedicated!

The stage coach road turned just beyond the tavern and went up what is now Melody Lane, coming out to the present route 10 just passed Walker Motor Sales!

It was called Haverhill Road and continued toward Bath, nearly to the present railroad trestle before turning sharply to Mill street, Hiland (Highland) street, Ammonoosuc street, all of which was ten called Haverhill Road, to the covered bridge! The road turned west before the bridge and continued down what is now South Court street as far as the building presently beyond the old Jimmy Rowe Farm.

Haverhill road stopped there, with just the length of the short field where Tegu's Meadows Drive later stood! In later years it was extended to the hospital and called South Court street!

## Roundhouses

Most of the early growth of Woodsville was due o the railroad and its many workers. They, obviously, needed housing and Mr. Whitcher was a big assist in that area. He operated a saw mill on, obviously, Mill street and had many homes built in Woodsville, which he sold at very reasonable prices and terms!

Many railroad workers were paid to help clear housing lots and many participated in the actual building of homes. The Railroad knew, in order to survive, it had to make Woodsville a community.

The first engine house in Woodsville was down near the toll house, and where the present Railroad Park is now located; offering a concert stage, walking trail and an expanding children's play area, with new things for them being added all the time!

Unfortunately it burned in 1907 and was never rebuilt. The engines were not removed because of a tragic event that is pictured in the following pages!

**Most of the engines that were housed in the sheds at time were restored.**

As far as the unfortunate damage to the engines in the sheds at the time of the fire ... it was caused by mistakes many of us would have made, if put into the situation one of the workers faced!

One very alert worker realized the extent of the fire and calculated the damage that was sure to occur. He instantly started up one of the engines and prepared to move it out of danger. Once accomplished he would continue removing engines until the sheds were empty!

Unfortunately, his alertness escaped him as he drove the first engine onto the turntable. He acted a bit too hastily, without checking the direction of the tracks on the turn table. Unfortunately they were not in line with the tracks from the stall he was exiting. Hence the following disaster, which made the removal of any more engines impossible!

I cannot start to describe how this loyal railroad worker must have felt. On the other hand, if he had been successful he would have become an instant hero!

Pictures on the follow few pages will attempt to show you the extent of the damage caused by this fire. I do not know where the fire started, but there are historical remnants down over the banking that should be made visible.

# Woodsville's Memorable Buildings

The newer engine house, early 1908, had a ten bay shed. It was surrounded by three sides forming the wye, which enabled the ability to direct traffic in any direction, or completely reverse the direction of a train.

I am pleased, and very grateful, that as a young boy to have driven an engine onto the very same turntable you see in the previous photo. I wasn't, however, allowed to drive it into it's shed!

The houses visible over the sheds are the ones, presently, above Shaw's Grocery store on Central and Forrest streets! This roundhouse was visible while walking across the 'dry Bridge' into Stoneville, if you looked over the fence along the sidewalk, on the north side of the bridge! Looking over the south side of the bridge you would see the lower yards!

**Sometimes there would be a hundred freight cars there, lined up ready to be sent back to where they came from.**

Top left in the above picture … Coal shed!

## Toll House

The Gallagher family was the first to operate the tolls across the double decker bridge. They were the toll keepers from the early 1890's until 1897 when the James A. Sawyer took over. The Sawyers were there until 1913.

New toll keepers took over in 1913. They were the Winfield Keysar family! The rates for tolls at that time (1905) were ... two cents for foot crossings on the sidewalk that was attached to the south side of the bridge.

Five cents for a horse and rider.

Five cents for a carriage or sleigh with one horse, with five cents additional for each extra horse.

One cent each for sheep or cattle.

Three cents for a bicycle and rider.

Twenty-five cents per automobile.

Once the free Rangers bridge was completed, there was no need for the toll house and it was sold to Lewis N. Wells, as a family home! In later years Ted Paradie and family lived here and Mr. Paradie operated a taxi service here, for many years!
There are no remains of the old toll house....

In January of 1961 the Atlantic and Pacific Company moved into it's new location just south of the old Toll House which had been removed and partially filled for a parking area for the new A&P store!

Depot

Passengers were at first accommodated, as to a waiting room, tickets, etc, in the Railway Express building, It was located just north of the building on the track side!

There were rows of luggage wagons, with large wheels that when parked by a freight car door, would be level with the car floor! Getting up on one, as a young lad, was a bit of a struggle. But, with a foot on the wheel spoke and a quick jump, and a well executed turn we would be safely seated!

We would sit by the hour watching people scrambling to transfer to another train, or they would run across the street to Charlie Christopher's store for a magazine, a cigar, or a news paper!

LUNCH STAND BETWEEN DEPOT AND RAILWAY EXPRESS BUILDING
CENTRAL STREET, WOODSVILLE, NEW HAMPSHIRE ... "JOIN SERVICE" 1940

The Service Flag waved over the street with the number of Haverhill men and women enlisted in the war, embroidered on a removable patch !

Freight packages, luggage, and items shipped were delivered by the Express Wagon.

*American Express wagon.*

*After the roundhouse fire in 1907.*

Boston & Maine Station, Woodsville, N. H.

# Woodsville's Memorable Buildings

Boston & Maine Station, Woodsville, N. H.

BOSTON & MAINE PASSENGER DEPOT, WOODSVILLE 1921 FIRE

PASSENGER DEPOT, WOODSVILLE NH

PASSENGER DEPOT, WOODSVILLE NH

# Woodsville's Memorable Buildings

**FLETCHER'S PAINT STORE IN THE OLD DEPOT**

**DEISEL IN WOODSVILLE**

# Woodsville's Memorable Buildings

BOSTON & MAINE PASSENGER DEPOT, WOODSVILLE, NEW HAMPSHIRE

EXPRESS WAGON AT WOODSVILLE, NH, DEPOT, JUNE of 1900
STANDING LEFT TO RIGHT Q.A. Scott, E.M. Markham, F.H. George, F.A. Layne, W. Pusham, and F.M. George

# Woodsville's Memorable Buildings

PEOPLE GATHERED BY TELEGRAPH OFFICE, DEPOT, WOODSVILLE, NEW HAMPSHIRE

MOTORCYCLE PARKED IN FRONT OF DEPOT, WOODSVILLE, NEW HAMPSHIRE

## THE FIREHOUSE

**Woodsville Fire Department ... 1887 was the year the New Hampshire legislature created the Woodsville Fire District. The original fire house was between the Methodist Church, the library, on the edge of the embankment overlooking South Court Street.**

**This building was moved to 101 Central Street, on the corner of Chapel and Central, now an auto repair garage.**

**1899**
**The cupola was hit by lightning in 1907.**

**A large annex was added in 1973. There were small hose houses built at various locations around town to enable quicker access to fire fighting equipment, in the event of a fire.**

One hose house was on School Street, by the library, another in the small building across from Shaw's Grocery Store's parking lot. The horse drawn wagons were slow arriving to fire scenes in outlying parts of town.

The hose reels were pulled by firemen, which was even slower. Obviously the availability of hoses in these small hose houses was sorely needed.

Year by year, as budgets allowed, hose, hydrants, and other advanced equipment were added to the fire department.

In 1885 about 500 feet of leather hose was purchased. It alone weighed over a ton. You can imagine how long it would take to move this much weight. And when a fire breaks out; time is most important!

A new hook and ladder wagon was purchased in 1892 and in 1894 another 400 feet of hose was added to the fire equipment inventory. In 1905 there were 24 hydrants in Woodsville.

The first motorized vehicle arrived in 1938 and in 1941 a trailer was made to carry the hose.

### 1906

The hook & ladder company, hose #1 and hose #2 are located in the Central Fire Station on Central and Chapel Streets (1915).

In 1941 the firemen built and maintained a hockey rink sized skating rink at the end of Connecticut Street, on the North end of the community field, between the baseball backstop and the last house on the east side of Connecticut Street. A new and much larger fire facility has now been built on Route 10, across from the new Walmart Store (2008)

Some of the major fires in Woodsville were the Mt. Gardner House in 1886, the first Odd Fellows Hall, Music Hall and stables in 1901, Mulliken Block Annex in 1906, the original railroad roundhouse by the double decker bridge in 1907 and the Parker House in 1912. The brick Odd Fellows Block on Pleasant Street in 1954, the elementary school in 1961, the Weeks (A&P) Block in 1961 and the Wentworth Hotel in 1969-70.

The Woodsville Fire Department's hose house got hit by lightening in 1907. This was the same year the first round house was destroyed by fire. The fire in the firehouse cupola was contained but there was some splintered wood damage.

### The Parker House

It is not known exactly when this building was built, but in 1872. John L. Davis purchased it after returning from serving in the Civil War! Mr. Davis also built the Mount Gardner House at 11–13 Central Street, in 1875–76. Unfortunately the building, down near the bowling alley, burned in 1886, and was never rebuilt!

The Parker House was built for Mrs. Hortense Ramsey as a boarding house, likely the first in Woodsville!

Mr. E. G. Parker started operating the Parker House in 1873, hence the name!

Mr. D. L. Hawkins and S. E. Nutting signed a five year lease for the the hotel in 1884. There were all kinds of events there in the following years, until the building was sold to Oscar D. Johnson, in 1887!

Mr. Johnson had several other enterprises in Woodsville during these early years!

THE PARKER HOUSE PRIOR TO 1890 WHEN THE TOP FLOOR WAS EXTENDED AND A FLAT ROOF ADDED

In 1898 the building was sold again. This time to Mr. Chester Abbott, one of the early land and building owners in Woodsville.

The Parker House had a large dining room and a livery stable to the rear of the main building. The stables burned when the first Odd Fellows Block was destroyed by fire in 1901!

The stables were replaced and the Parker House continued as a viable business until February of 1912, when the main building was completely destroyed by fire!

... replaced, a year later by Henderson Hotel.

I guess this would be a good time to segway into the next building, or the building now standing on the original Parker House lot ...... The Henderson Hotel!

Mr. Henderson contracted with James Lowe, well-known for moving buildings, to move a warehouse building moved from across the street, as the location of the Palace Theatre, which later became the Woodsville Bowling Alley!

Mr. Henderson's project was across the street from the Toll house and overlooked the Rangers Bridge. Has anyone ever wondered why that, our first non-toll bridge, was named that?

It was named after another prevaricator, not dissimilar to our local dictator! But that is another entire book, so let us move on to local historical facts!

Mr. Henderson purchased the burned out lot of the Parker House and constructed the finest hotel ever, in Woodsville! He moved his movie house here and later sold it to Peter Tegu who operated it has the Orpheum Theater!

Pete ran a popcorn machine between Spoffords Drug store and the Weeks block, in later years!

I still remember hearing Pete say, when I entered their home on School street ...."Jiminy Cricket!" That's what he always called me...........

Across the street from the theater was the Dandy Diner. My friend, Doc Blaisdell, gave me the following picture, and many others!

The photo was only two inches wide and all that was visible was a white sign saying 'EAT'! Doc had a little smirk on his face when he handed it to me. I had a smirk on my face when I handed the following back to him, after working on the small photo for two months, off and on! He was amazed at the results and had a big smile on his face when I said the new pic was for him!

DANDY DINER and TEGU'S ORPHEUM THEATER ADVERTISING TRUCK, WOODSVILLE, NH

#1117-001          43 CENTRAL STREET, WEST OF B&M DEPOT          COPYRIGHT 2006 BEAU DANGLES STUDIO

The top floor of People's Market, down on No. Court street, through the underpass, is visible to the right!

Let's see, where was I! I think I was about to tell about the Henderson Hotel! Let's do just that!

The first business' to open in this hotel were Kugelman's store and King Cafe! His theater was in the middle, but there was no marquee, as yet!

Edward J. King operated the café here in 1915 and lived in St. Johnsbury, Vt. It is doubtful he was related to the King family that owned one of the first houses in Woodsville, on Cheney Corner. They owned the farm on South Court street that, in my time, was the Rowe farm!

The family also owned most of the 500 acres of the Governors Farm; Woodsville! The King family donated the land for the high school, hence King's Plain in the school song!

The store on the left was owned by Levi Kugelman, who operated a clothing store in Woodsville.

In later years the store was run by Robert, the son of Levi and Rosa Kugelman. They evidently started  at 3 Pleasant street, the annex to the Weeks Block. They then opened as the first retailer in the new Henderson block!

The Kugelman store later moved to their last location which was in the Glover-Gibson-Spofford block at 83 Central street, now the business of the Shadow Box Art & Framing where you can purchase art supplies or have your prints or paintings expertly matted and/or framed!

### Hotel Wentworth

Now ... here is a building well worth discussing! Many people could certainly tell you more about the Wentworth than I can, but here we go.

I have this picture posted in my store. Many people have asked the following question. "Do you ever remember going into this place?"

My answer never varies! I say, "I always remember going in. Coming out however, is a bit foggy!"

There were times, in the Wentworth, that weren't as calm and serene as in this picture. My grandfather, Ted Hobbs, was the chief of Police from the early 1940's until 1955.

There would be a kerfuffle of one kind, or another, most every weekend. Either laid over railroad men or loggers, or both would get into a fight and a regular local might join in, just for the hellovit.

After a pint, or two, an ant might look sideways at someone and all of a sudden the chairs would start flying, tables would start flipping over, and a chair, or two, would go orbital!

Pa would be called to the riot! He would walk right thru the middle of the battle field directly to the bar. He would then pull a small leather blackjack out of his back pocket, and slam it two or three times on the bar!

You could hear a powder puff drop! The room was like when a movie would get stuck on a single frame at the Orpheum theater!

Back at the fight ... Pa would point at a couple of known trouble makers that would fight at the drop of a hat and motion them to leave.

Once outside he would load them into his 1950 Hudson, that was our unmarked family car, and he would take them home!

Them was tha' good ole days!

Another time Pa was leaning against the wood fence in front of Dave Riggi's mens shop, waiting for someone to come out of the Wentworth and head toward a parked truck loaded with Christmas trees!

A man, later, strolled out and started toward the truck. Pa asked if it was his truck, The man said it was and the trees were legal. Pa said that was fine, but why are they bleeding!

There was a puddle of blood on the street. They had three deer under the trees! Such was crime in this town!

One another occasion a man pulled up in from of the hotel, proud  as a peacock of the deer he had tied to his front fender. Pa wasn't pleased about that either! His deer was small, white, with tiny horns. It would have said, "Blat, Blat"! if it had spoken in time. Blat, blat in animal talk is, "Don't shoot, you idiot ... I'm a goat!"

Robert Frost, supposedly wrote about the Wentworth in his book, "Hundred Collars. Frost called the hotel the Poor Man's Inn!

Speaking of deer reminds me of the shop class Spider Hubbard and I took in out freshman year at WHS.

A farmer ask for us to make him a full sized deer out of two inch wood. He even gave us a set of antlers to attach to it! We cut the thing out, painted it and attached the antlers. The farmer came and picked it up. He was very happy with it!

He placed it in his field out in Swiftwater. The road was full of cartridges shortly after and our deer was so full of holes you could see right through it! What does that have to do with the Wentworth Hotel, you ask! Not a damned thing!

# Woodsville's Memorable Buildings

## CHILDHOOD MEMORIES

Entering elementary school in Woodsville was not the highlight of my life! Mainly because the teacher in North Haverhill always walked me home, and in Woodsville she did not!

North Haverhill

Woodsville

My mother finally got sick of pushing me thru the front door and my running thru the halls and out the back door. getting back home before she did, and threatened to give me a licking! I said, "Beat me all you want as long as I don't have to go to that school!"

A few days later I meet Bobby Hubbard, George Chase, Bernard Roy, Bob's Daniels and Savoy, and I forgot all about the North Haverhill school!

We played kick-a-ball and basketball by the hour. Summer evenings there would be 25-30 kids, of all sizes and ages, all playing together!

There were many times there was a rim shot and the basketball would be heading by the library, down School street, between the Tegu and Batjaika houses, passing Toodie Hoods' and then it would make the turn down Clay Hill toward the Community Field!

I finally discovered it was easier to climb through the hole in the wire fence, slide down the banking to the driveway of the Veayo house and wait there for the ball to arrive!

Climbing back up the banking was a bit more difficult!

The Walkers lived at that time on Chapel street. We would play basketball there in the winter. Dribbling a basketball in slush is not pleasant. The slush would splash up onto our trousers and then freeze.

Jimmy Walker's mother knew what time each of us were supposed to be home and would come out on the side porch and let us know. Jimmy Walker was a little younger than us. But, we let him play. What the hell, it was his backboard!

Once we got up into 5th and 6th grades we were able to kick the ball over the street into the yard of the Episcopal church. The stables were still there at that time!

The opening between the church and the stables was our path to the Kelley store! There was a fire about that time in the Kelley, Bill Hartwell building. They were back in business real soon and offered a super ice cream cone. It was a cylinder shaped scoop and the cone would hold two scoops side by side. You could even choose two different flavors!

Who the hell needs a cell phone when you can shoot hoops for a couple hours and then enjoy a double scoop ice cream cone!

There were many events for kids put on by St. Lukes' Parish house, including dances. The porch was open at that time and there were benches all around the perimeter of the hall. I believe they still hold dinners in the basement!

I remember one time, before the porch was closed in, of going to a special town meeting. I was about 18 at the time and working at McAllister Jewelers in the Opera Block!

I opened the door to see the backs of very tall people. I squiggled and pushed and finally inched myself far enough into the room to be able to close the door. The meeting was about allowing sweepstakes tickets to be sold in New Hampshire.

One of the town fathers was telling how, if this was adopted, it would put an end to school taxes! I think they meant to say it would put an end to *low* school taxes!

I remember asking the Chairman of the Select Board for a tiny favor, one time, after a Heritage meeting. The favor was so insignificant that I can't even remember what it was! He said he wouldn't help because he was dedicated only to the property tax payers! Sometimes people in high places should look down to people in lower places! They vote too!

My grandfather, Chief of Police Edward G. Hobbs, died when I was a senior in high school. He didn't even have social security! That left my mother and grandmother and I with the big house on South Court street.

I contributed, as best I could, with my paycheck from McAllister's Jewelers. I made $1.00 an hour at that time. Gas was less than a quarter. Cigarettes were sixteen cents a pack, and so on. But, $40.00 a week didn't help much as far as how much I could put toward the taxes.

Years later my brother didn't always have ample tax money on our place on Airport road. So, I helped when I could. After his death I moved back from Florida where I was retired and the estate paid the taxes!

So, when I was told he wouldn't consider helping me out, and I wasn't asking for money at all, I still get a sour taste in my mouth when I think back at that comment, while he is requesting thousands of dollars for a survey on Powder Puff Hill!

I promised my self I would not get politics involved in this my 307th book. I guess I broke my promise!

I do not have a picture of the Kelley store, unfortunately! But I do have many memories and a picture of the Rowden block where Kelley and Hartwell would later be located!

THE ROWDEN BLOCK

Fred Mann's Store In the Rowden Block!

On August 31st, 1912, Chester Abbotts hotel that operated using many different names from Brunswick Hotel, to the Central House, The Guilford and finally the Tremont House ... burned to the ground with a strong suspicion it was arson!

The Methodist church had already moved up a street to Maple and avoided any damage from the fire! However St. Lukes did receive some fire damage!

No one in the Tremont was hurt which was lucky because even with a large decline in business there were still people there! Then came a new owner. The lot was cleared of debris and a two story building was but up by a Mr. Thomas Rowden. There were two store spaces on the street level, Mr. William (Bill) Hartwell was on one side and Fred Mann in the other. Bill Hartwell had been in business in the Lovejoy block, as had the Siprelle family, with a photo studio. Siprelle had taken most of the school class pictures for many years!

Fred Mann's store was on the left side facing the building. As per the previous picture you can see he had a good mix of needed items at that point in time!

Guy and Lorene Kelley bought out the Mann store in the early 1940's, just about the time we moved here from North Haverhill! Guy Kelley was not a new comer to business in Woodsville. He worked in the Opera Block in his fathers business in 1900!

Guy and Lorene took over the Mann portion of the building and in 1945 Mr. Rowden sold the building to Harold Taylor, who turned around and sold it to the Kelleys in 1950!

Fire hit the area again in 1950 and destroyed most of the interior of the Rowden Block, actually the Kelley block! The Kelleys were not the 'give up' kind and practically overnight had the interior rebuilt into one large; Kelley's One Stop Shop.

This store continued under the management of Guy, Jr. Other owners, through the years ran it as a store until in November of 1973 it turned into Chamberlin's Flower Shop!

At 151 Central street the home of James Powers stood, a bit back from the sidewalk, as I recall. The building was torn down by Freddie Grenier and the materials were used to build a camp in Newbury!

Once it became a clear building lot Dick Paradie opened Dick's American Service and operated as such until the mid 1960. Cumberland Farms Petco Minimart opened in 1973 and the building is presently available, as they have moved to the upper part of town across from Shaw's Grocery!

I just found a picture of the Henderson theater before Pete Tegu purchased it!

I seem to be drifting up and down Central street without any plan at all! But, if you have read any of my other books you are likely used to it!

A while back I mentioned the wooden rail fence along the tracks. Here is a pic from 1890!

This pic from in front of Doc Eastman's, with a dirt road that must have been great during mud season, which was, likely, most of the time. Mix that with some of the material horses tended to leave behind back then and you've got your self some smelly muddy boots!

That would not be unique back then! Even the sidewalk in that pic appear to be just plain dirt. I guess Mr. Tilton's sidewalk paving company was just getting started!

I have to tell you something funny! At least I think it is hilarious! But then, if you know me you are aware what I think is funny is not always that to others!

Like the other day when I was heading to the Copy Store in Wells River. When I started across the Memorial bridge, which replaced the Ranger bridge, there were people lined up the entire length of the bridge.

As I headed down the slope to the railroad trestle I saw a tour bus refueling! That's when it came to me. They were leaf peepers! They all had their cameras out, obviously taking pictures south of the bridges.

They were taking pictures of the island down by the Community Field, thinking it was No Man's Island, I assume! At one time there was no sign of an island there!

Some weeds and trash got caught when the river was low. As time went by more dirt and silt and likely some seeds of some kind got hung up there, and practically right before our island was born!

You would think with all of the brainiacs presently running this town, that someone would think that, perhaps, just by chance, we might possibly be better off if tour busses got the hint that we have No Man's Island, the Covered Bridge, and the narrows, all within one square mile!

Naw! That's too easy! Let's just add a few more beauty shops and nail salons. Hows that working out so far? Plus something could be done promoting the double decker bridge, the old roundhouse stones, the water pump house that is still in amazingly good condition, except for needing a roof!

Hell No! Instead we put in flower pots, dog-crap receptacles, and park benches! At least the druggies have a place to sit down while they shoot up and dry out, ready for the next fix! Oh, that's right, they don't have any money! Lock your doors or else you will, likely, be the next to donate to their cause!

I've already given ...... $7,000.00!!

Speaking of the Narrows, how long do you think it took to make it! I was told Nelson Chamberlain was heading toward property he had toward Monroe when a deer came flying off the ledges at the Narrows and handed on the hood of his truck. It was, likely being chased by dogs and ran out of space!

This pic is from the early 1930's! You would think floods would have wiped out the fences! They say there are Northern Pike in there that could haul you off! There are, also, Cusk Eels, so I am told !

Cusk Eel

There aren't many people alive that remember the flood of 1927. So, there are not many people around that either danced or played music for dancers, at the dance pavilion on No Man's Island.

Supposedly there is a photograph somewhere that shows the piano from the dance pavilion, as it is floating under the bridge! I have digital copies of 15 - 20 thousand vintage pictures of towns in New Hampshire and Vermont.

I have a file of way over a thousand pictures of Woodsville alone! Someone was in a couple of weeks ago who has dozens of old pictures of Wells River. Sooner or later they may show up!

The island, itself, is smaller than it was in the early part of the century and most believe it was, at one time, a peninsula! In the summer of 1899 Mr. P. J. Haley erected the dance pavilion on the island!

The pavilion was more like a three sided shelter! There was a walking bridge from the Vermont side to the island! Midway on the bridge was a partition stretching out enough distance to keep people from   entering the island when it was closed. There was a lock on the door!

The cement mooring for the bridge is still in place! I slid down the embankment to take a picture of it one day. I had to grab small trees and large bushes in order to climb back up to the embankment! Just as I was about to find something to grab onto enabling me to get to the path; the enormous head of a German Shepherd peered down at me. It was growling! I looked down and all I saw was water and rocks below!

So I just froze there, hoping the dog would go home! In a few minutes a man approached and called the dog off. I asked him why the dog wasn't on a leash.

He asked why I wasn't on a leash! He said he didn't expect to see anyone here! I didn't get into it with him. He had a dog! The only thing I had was goose bumps!

Mike Dannehy and I were on the north end of the area near the sandy spot. We were looking down river toward the Memorial bridge. I thought I saw something and pointed it out to Mike. We soon realized it was a large Buck! Following right behind was a doe, and then, swimming like hell, head pointing toward the sky, was a 7-8 month old fawn!

The embankment on the Vermont side, at that point, is nearly straight up! They all made it in a manner that looked to be effortless!

Whatever song they were playing back in 1927 was the last song coming from the dance hall!

**GOING GOING GONE!**

**Back in the day, horse and wagon or horse and buggy were an everyday thing.   Not so much, these days!**

**The Express Wagon**

**Rolling the snowy streets!**

## Rolling the streets

## Peddling Water!

Buggy by depot

Mann & Mann Delivery

**Miller's Ice Wagon**

**Ice Delivery**

## The Lovejoy Block

107-111 Central street

After serving during the Civil War, Wellington H. Lovejoy became an Indian-fighter. I do not know what the exact description of an Indian fighter is, but that is up to others to deside. Wellington arrived in Woodsville sometime in 1896!

He was in the meat business originally in the Odd Fellows Music Hall building, between the Odd Fellows block and the Weeks block on the corner of Main and Pleasant streets!

Within a year he purchased a lot up Main (Central) street, by what later became Doc Eastman's house. The Eastman lot was likely baron at that time, with a dirt road running parallel with the railroad tracks!

## Doctor Eastman's home

The Eastman house was originally built in 1890 for railroad man, G. C. Cummings.

Lovejoy put up a two story building and operated his meat market in the space on the left side, facing the building!

In the later 1800'e he did some remodeling of the building and moved his meat business to the street level, giving him more rental space. His meat market would be where Julius Tueckhardt later, much later, operated his newspaper!

In the early 1900's the Deacon installed electric lights and telephone service! Wellington was called Deacon because he was very religious and later went into the ministry!

**Wellington Lovejoy's building was also beside the Brunswick Hotel!**

Mr. Lovejoy retired in 1905! The meat business was bought out by William 'Bill' Hartwell. After the hotel fire in 1913, a new block was erected. This block became the new home for Bill Hartwell. The first A&P Store was located in the opposite side of the Rowden block from 1914 until 1919.

The Rowden block later became the home for several different ladies dress shops, which were very popular during that time!

Millinery and dress shops became very popular for many years. Later, in the early 1920's the Rowden Block housed the Haverhill Shoe store, from Massachusetts.

The ladies dress shops opened, closed, changed hands, and so on for many of the years in the early 1920's! Of them were: Miss Cutting, Miss Bowen (Taplin), Miss K. D. Whitcher, Mrs. K. D. Shepherd, Mrs. W. D. Ashley, Mrs. Vernia L. Carpenter as Woodsville Millinery Company, Mrs. C. H. Burkinshaw, Charlotte Nutter, Miss M. L. Goslant-Baker, Mrs. M. L. Burnham, Esther and Phoebe Nutter as the Vogue Song and Gift Shop!

M. Bowen Taplin's shop in the Rowden block!

Back to the Lovejoy building; in 1925 the Siprelle family purchased the Lovejoy building and operated a photo studio there for many years! In 1942 the building and studio was sold to Winthrop Klark, a photographer.

It remained a photographic business up into the late 1950's as George Scheller's studio and is presently home for the Antique Rose!

## Davison Hall

This building was located in the back lot of the home now owned by Norman Darby at 129 Central street. Not many people in Woodsville had a building in their back yard!

How and why this happened is easy to explain and I will attempt to do just that, if you are patient!

In the early days in the settlement of Woodsville; the schools were quickly out grown. The first school house was at the base of Clay hill.

As you can see it was, merely, a little home, and when it got outgrown, it became someone else's little home! This was the first and last time that every happened!

The next school for obvious reasons, was a much larger building, that even though over estimated as to the student growth, was useful for a number of years.
And then, it too had been outgrown!

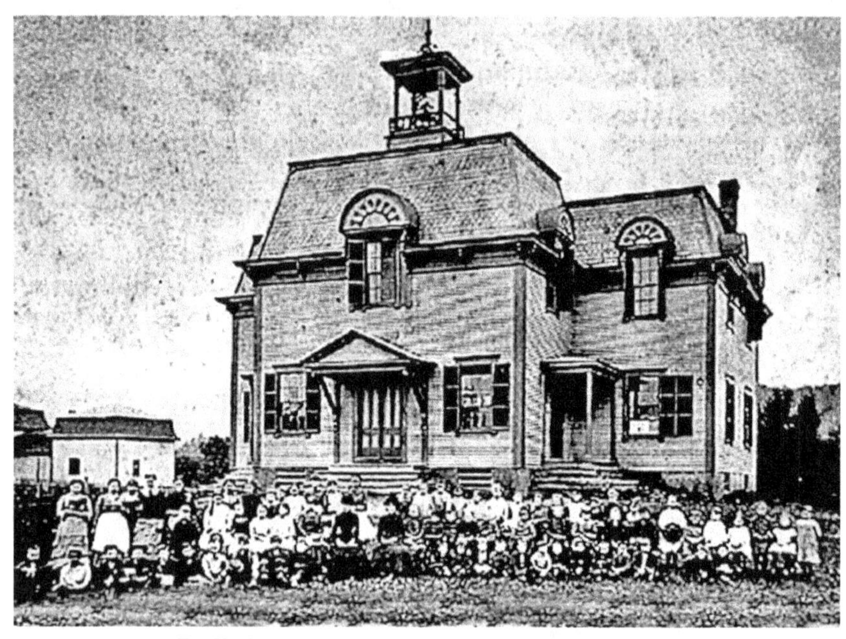

Built in 1872 and replaced in 1899

The old school was moved by into the back yard owned by C.  N. Davison, a former railroad employee. Classes continued as normal until the Christmas break when the new school was finished! After the Christmas break classes continued in the new school!
Mr.  Davison was interested in turning the building into tenements, but businesses started to inquire immediately about renting spaces on the street level floor and Davison took advantage of those requests by renting space.

The first renters were Mr. N. B. Perkins and Rhrett Scruggs who had purchased the plumbing and sheet metal business previously in the Mulliken Block!

These entrepreneurs started this new business that was, initially listed as "N. B. Perkins & Co." In 1906, it seems they evidently had some internal problems. That sometimes happens when two friends become partners!

Mr. Perkins moved, for some unknown reason, to Montreal, selling his share of the business to Mr. Scruggs. Rhett Scruggs continued doing business in the Davison building until hr moved into the Brick Block in 1910!

In 1907 Mr. Davison moved his bakery out of the Odd Fellows Block on Pleasant street to his own building, calling it Woodsville Bakery. In later years it was called Woodsville Bakery and Up-town Grocery Store!

In 1912 Mr. Cyrus Cameron moved his furniture store from Wells River to the Davison building! His business, evidently, didn't flourish so he sold it to Woodsville Furniture Company in the Odd Fellows Block!

Scruggs had moved into the Brick Block so Davison removed the partition previously dividing the room, and expanded his own store, offering a delivery service by wagon.

Mr. Davison, evidently, was a generous person, because he let out the upstairs for high school events and other function, at no charge!

I have heard a man from St. Johnsbury came to Davison Hall, likely in the up stairs and showed movies. The Moose Lodge used the upstairs part of Davison Hall, for a period of time around 1925-1926.

A promoter used the upstairs to hold his wrestling matches!

Then the building out lived its usefulness and Bill Brill tore it down and hauled off the material, some of  which was used to rebuild his home that was destroyed by fire in 1941!

## Woodsville Free Library

In 1871 the Ladies Charitable Society set out to create a library. Charles B. Drake was appointed as the librarian and was placed in charge of the fews books they had been able to purchase.

The Woodsville Free Library was formed In 1894 and the books were turned over to them. Mr. Ira Whitcher donated the land for, and erected, the present library! Mr. Whitcher had a lumber mill on Mill street and owned quite a bit of land in Woodsville.

Mr. Whitcher was a most generous person. Along with the land and building he also donated a thousand dollars worth of books!

## The Haverhill-Bath Covered Bridge

There are not many children in Woodsville, back in the 50's and earlier, that didn't learn how to swim under the covered bridge. We swam there. We fished there. We caught turtle there. We played there! You might say the covered bridge was the entertainment center for kids, back in the day!

Logs were dynamited when they jammed up during a log drive, under the bridge!

The power plant and Woodsville Creamery were located on the lower part of the bridge, just before the Ammonoosuc joined the Connecticut river.

Anything built near a river is bound too flood, sooner, or later!

## Power Plants flood too!

## They catch on fire, Too!

The creamery was opened on January 1st, 1901 and in 1904 was sold to Lyndonville Creamery and operated until the mid 1930's. The building was removed and a storage building for the power plant was built!

The first industry in Woodsville was here and operated by Mr. Woods. A Dam and saw mill was here before Mr. Woods arrived on the scene. The first mill was run by Mr. Cotton around 1910-11, and later by Mr. Mills Olcott a few years later.

Mr. Woods leased the property for awhile before purchasing it in 1830. Mr. Woods put in a grist mill and a saw mill before selling out to Charles B. Smith who manufactured shovel handles! Mr. Smiths mill and dam washed out in 1878 and Mr. Smith passes away in 1880, before he was able to replace them!

Charles Smith had been the postmaster from 1873 until 1880. Mr. Smith's son Henry, ran a saloon nearby that later became People's Market!

Woodsville Aquaduct Company was incorporated in 1885. The railroad owned 1/3 of the stock. The Aquaduct Co. purchased rights to Mr. Woods mill, built a new dam and installed pumping equipment. Up until 1969 they generated the electricity for the town.

## Logging and Log Drives

The place, or people, that likely knew what was going on in a log drive, more than anyone else, were the people on a wanigan. I am sure you know what a wanigan is, so I won't go into a long definition.

What! You do not know what it is! Well, now, you are likely the only person in this galaxy that doesn't!

I was certain everyone knew that! The wanigan I am speaking of went by the name ... Mary Ann!

No! It is not another name you call an old boyfriend or girlfriend!  The Mary Ann I am talking about is a house boat! She, the Mary Ann, travelled with a log drive supplying meals to the loggers, and by the following picture may have done a bit of laundry!

It is a house on a raft that was built in sections so it could be easily disassembled in places like the Narrows on the Connecticut river just north of Woodsville.

The Mary Ann might, also, have to be partly, or totally, torn down before facing rapids or water falls! In extremely hot weather the sides could be removed allowing the breeze from the river to be used for air conditioning!

There are two white cap and apron cooks on the Mary Ann! They do not have the normal serving hours. They make five to seven meal servings a day. That doesn't even take in accounting the number of meals that are sent down river for meals for the front crews!

The recipes are a bit different on the Mary Ann as compared to home cooking. As an example; the material for making Biscuits are quite different from how your Granny made them. On the Mary Ann the pan for mixing the dough is about the size of a bushel basket and the stirring spoon looks more like a canoe paddle!

One of my most favorite pictures is that of a logger preparing to ride a log down over the dam by the power plant. I used to swim exactly where the logger is positioned!

One of the biggest problems in log drives was that we had the Ammonoosuc and the Connecticut rivers; both emptying logs into the Connecticut in Woodsville at the same time.

Doc. Blaisdell once showed me a length of huge chain. He said it was the chain they placed across both rivers before they joined at the covered bridge.

It was a rotational agreement between the two lumber companies. At a certain time, the chain would be drawn across one of the rivers This would hold the logs back at that point. After a agreed upon day, or time, the chain would de drawn across the other river and the first one pulled back allowing the logs to proceed downstream!

I am sure there must have been a certain time period, because there would be tremendous log jams if they were held too long!

James E. Henry was one of the larger log drives. The following information was taken, with permission, about Mr. Henry!

****************

### James E. Henry
### Wood Butcher or Just a Good Businessman?
### by Rick Russack

James E. Henry is one of the more controversial characters in the history of the White Mountains. He was roundly criticized in the press of the day for his logging methods. He was called a "wood butcher" because his logging crews engaged in "clear cutting". That refers to the practice of cutting all trees on a piece of land, not cutting selectively, as is now done.

A consequence of Henry's clear cutting was that his lands were littered with "slash"- the tops and branches of trees that were not used for lumber or pulp.

Slash was fuel for forest fires and there were large fires on Henry's lands.  However, when judging Henry and his methods it must be remembered that the science of forestry did not exist when he was logging.  He did what most others did but he did it on a larger scale.

Henry built two towns and over 50 miles of logging railroads. He built saw mills, pulp mills and paper mills. Although a shrewd businessman, his employees were loyal and considered themselves well treated.  In many families, more than one generation worked for the Henrys.

From humble beginnings, J.E. Henry and his three sons would eventually own thousands of acres of woodland, ranging from Crawford Notch, through the Pemi Wilderness, to Lincoln and Franconia. At various times, he operated saw mills from the Lower Falls of the Ammonoosuc down to Livermore Falls on the Campton/Plymouth line. He owned a saw mill and charcoal kiln on lands he sold to the Mt. Pleasant Hotel Co.

Mr. Henry owned part of the land the Mt. Washington Hotel is built on.  Eventually, most of the land he owned became part of the White Mountain National Forest.

J.E. Henry was born in 1831 in Lyman, NH and the first years of his life were spent on a farm.  His father died in 1845, and supporting the family became his responsibility.

Farming income was supplemented with driving a freight wagon through Crawford Notch to Portland, and probably with the sale of timber from small wood lots.

He married in 1854, and continued to earn his living from a variety of occupations.  The first of five children, a daughter, was born in 1855. Eventually there would be two daughters and three sons.

The sons were all active in the business and were partners with their father. The Henry family moved a number of times in the early years. by 1872 it would appear that logging was the main business.

Grafton County deeds indicate that in 1875 J.E. Henry acquired his first part ownership of a sawmill, near Fabyans. He had a number of partnerships over the next few years, bought and sold much timberland, and eventually, by 1881, had bought out all his partners and was operating his own steam powered saw mill in Zealand.

Charcoal was a major product for Henry and it appears that he operated charcoal kilns at three different locations. Probably the first was on land that he eventually sold to the Mt. Pleasant Hotel. Early maps of the area show a trail known as "Coal Kiln Trail". Remnants of a large kiln have recently been found in that area. This kiln was probably discontinued when Henry began to operate in Zealand, in 1880.

Mr. Henry had kilns in Zealand and Lincoln. Remnants, although difficult to find, remain in Zealand. In Lincoln, it's believed that the kilns were slightly to the east of Pollard Brook where it crosses Rt. 112. No evidence remains of these kilns but photos survive.

In 1885, he began building and operating the Zealand Valley Railroad. He built a town with 2 railroad stations, a large modern steam sawmill, a boarding house, post office, store, homes for workers, a large home for himself, and the five charcoal kilns.

The logging railroad eventually extended several miles into the virgin timberland and millions of board feet of lumber were cut in the Zealand Valley.

By 1892, the accessible timber had been cut. He leased his Zealand mill and some equipment to a business associate, George Van Dyke and it was time to move on to Lincoln.

When Henry and his men arrived in Lincoln, the town we know today as Lincoln did not exist. Where the Village Shops, homes, hotels, restaurants, condominiums, and a ski area now exist, there was nothing but trees. And more trees.

The population in 1892 was 110 and the town was located along the road to Franconia Notch.

Lincoln, under the Henrys, was truly a company town. The Henrys built the sawmill, homes for the workers, a store, a hospital, a hotel, boarding houses, a post office, churches, and perhaps most importantly, a very well built logging railroad.

As the larger trees were cut, and paper making technology improved, the Henry family built pulp mills and sold the pulp to paper mills. After a few years, paper making machinery was added, and high-grade papers were produced until 1980 (under a variety of corporate ownerships).

James Henry and his sons, at one time or another, held all of Lincoln's major offices: selectmen, tax collector, justice of the peace, etc. When the mills were converted to use electricity, the entire town was supplied by the company.

The East Branch and Lincoln Railroad survived almost 50 years. It was the longest and probably best built of the many White Mountain logging railroads. The roadbeds are still in use today for hiking, and vestiges of the log camps can still be seen. Henry also invested in hotels. He owned Thayers Hotel in Littleton for a short time around 1901 and may have been a part owner of the White Mountain House near his Zealand mills.

J.E. Henry, his wife Eliza, and his three sons, George, John and Charles

James E. Henry died in 1912.  In 1917, his sons sold the company, and the town, to The Parker Young Company, for $3,000,000. The Parker Young Co. had been established in Lisbon, NH in the mid-1870s; they were a well-established wood products company.

The public criticism of loggers like J.E. Henry and his contemporaries had significant positive results. The most important of these was the eventual passage of the Weeks Act, in 1911, which authorized the Federal government to purchase privately owned forest land.

It was the Weeks Act that allowed the creation of the White Mountain National Forest.

Additional information on J.E. Henry can be found at our related site, LoggingInLincoln.com

Suggested Reading:

J.E. Henry's Logging Railroads by Bill Gove

****************************

Local Train Wrecks

I realize train wrecks are not a pleasant subject, and even less pleasant when life is lost. However; these events are a part of our local history and should be on record as equally important as our memorable buildings.

Some of our other buildings, actually many of our memorable buildings, are railroad buildings. The first engine houses, the Express building, the depots ... plus many bridges and trestles are because of the railroad!

One such incident happened in the lower engine house yards in 1921. I do not have much information as to why this happened.

This accident ended with the death of Frank Pain.

This wreck was in 1931, the engineer scalded, happened just a block away from my store.....

**The most tragic wreck happened when the engine and a couple of cars went tumbling off the railroad trestle just south of the Twin River Lodge, below Bath, NH.  It was the wreck at Rum Hill Bridge!**
**It ended up in the Ammonoosuc river!**
**1897**

ENGINE 601 WRECKED OFF RUM HILL BRIDGE, NORTH OF WOODSVILLE, NH, 7-6-1897
HERBERT GALE, CONDUCTOR .. PATRICK LEMMON, ENGINEER .. O. E. LANG & EUGENE CLARK, BRAKEMAN
HERBERT PEBBLES, FIREMAN   ...   ALL BUT GALE DIED IN THE WRECK

**New Hampshire  * Train Wrecks and Accidents I**
**1897**

## THREE KILLED IN A WRECK.

**Cloudburst Causes a Washout on the Boston and Maine Railroad.**

**WOODSVILLE, N.H., July 6.---**A freight train on the White Mountain Division of the Boston and Maine Railroad was wrecked by a washout at a point four miles north of this station early this morning. Three men were killed and the engine and three cars were Patrick Lennon, engineer, Whitefield, N. H.; Bert Pebbles, fireman, Woodsville; O. E. Lange, brakeman, Berlin, New Hampshire.

The washout was caused by a cloudburst, which passed over this section yesterday. A great volume of water fell in a short time, and the small streams overflowed the lowlands.

The New York Times, New York, NY 7 Jul 1897

**************

### Fort Wellington

I'll wrap this up with a true or false, or better yet, Believe it or not.....................
Supposedly Rogers Rangers, did at one time, on his way back from a massacre in Canada, did stop at No Mans Island, in the Connecticut river, between Woodsville, NH and Wells River, Vt.
There is some evidence that the Rangers did pass through, at least that is what the marker states, that is by the turn off on route 10, just south of Woodsville and slightly north of the Grafton County Farm! While the hell it is stuck there, at least two miles south of No Mans Island, befuddles me!

But, everyone knows I am easily befuddled! But, befuddled or not, I am, according to our Select Board chairman, the only know living honorary member of the Haverhill Heritage Commission. And, I doubt if a person of his stature would lie, ................... again!

Then there is Lieutenant Colonel Robert Rogers, perhaps an even bigger liar than other 'Leaders' of the free world and everyone knows ..... nuttin' is free!

********

## St. Francis Raid
### From Wikipedia, the free encyclopedia

The St. Francis Raid was an attack in the French and Indian War by Robert Rogers on St. Francis, near the southern shore of the Saint Lawrence River in what was then the French province of Canada, on October 4, 1759.

Rogers and about 140 men entered the village, which was reportedly occupied primarily by women, children, and the elderly, early that morning, slaughtered many of the inhabitants where they lay, shot down many who attempted to flee, and then burned the village. Rogers reported killing as many as 300 people, while French reports placed the number closer to thirty, mainly women and children. One of Rogers' men was killed, and seven were wounded.

Rogers and his men endured significant hardships to reach the village from the British base at Fort Crown Point in present-day New York, and even more hardship afterwards. Chased by the French and vengeful Indians, and short on rations, Rogers and his men returned to Crown Point via the Connecticut River valley. Missteps in caching food stores for the expedition's use led to starvation, and some of Rogers' men were reportedly driven to cannibalism in order to survive.

About one third of the raid's participants did not return. British colonial reports of the raid were unapologetic, as St. Francis had long been a place from which the natives raided colonial settlements as far south as Massachusetts, and Rogers reported a large number of English scalps decorating the main village buildings.

Oral history of this debacle is much different from the previous! Oral history involves recording or transcribing eyewitness accounts of historical events. Some anthropologists started collecting recordings (at first especially of Native American folklore) on phonograph cylinders in the late 19th century.

I find a difference between 30 killed and Roberts count of 300 trophies, quite remarkable! But, if one listens to local leaders, which is in one way or another a matter of history; I find the outrageous lies about the same as those told by Rogers!

Fortunately the lies by our select board ruler do not, as yet, have anything to do with anyone being massacred. At least, not yet!

The way things are going in Haverhill, with elections that were not listed on any agenda, members voting for themselves, outlandish bias toward long standing local citizens that may have a different point of view to express ... might be misconstrued as being like a dictatorship! Perhaps Hitler isn't dead! Or, worse yet, perhaps he miss planted some seeds in Mexico and they migrated to America!

Skipping back to Rogers raid. Hasn't anyone ever seen a Hopalong Cassedy or Roy Rogers movie? Hell, Lee Tegu and I saw everyone at least 5 times! And I remember seeing the wagon train weaving along with high cliffs on each side. I also remember getting a quick glimpse of an Indian warrior, sitting on his horse, war spear by his side, feathers swaying in the breeze; watching......... Let's compare that scene with the same situation with 140 of Rogers' men, in boats, paddling up the river........

Don't you think, perhaps, an indian, yes I said Indian instead of Native American, would likely be perched as a lookout both below and above their village on the river! Ya think!

Perhaps that is why most of the villagers had fled before the mighty warrior, Rogers, arrived.

***********************

I have many friends in Woodsville and Wells River that are in business. I do not hesitate to put a good word for them in everything I publish. If they have read any of my books they may not be grateful for the free advertising!

On the other side of the coin I don't hesitate in giving a shop to those that mistreat people!

The word is I will be escorted out of Walmart should I attempt to ever enter their domain again. It seems they are not happy with an altercation I had with three employees while trying to return a faulty phone.

It took not one, not two, but three absolute nitwits in order to return the faulty phone. It was, they said, not returnable for a refund because I didn't have the box! The box was hanging on a rack and was destroyed when I opened it. Besides, I couldn't have called anyone with that friggin' box anyway!

It went something like this. I walked up to two employees at the return counter. One was a female, the other wasn't! I said I wanted to return the phone. They didn't say a word to me. The just whispered to each other. Some kind of a secret, I assume.

The female, the one on my left, evidently told the other, the one on the right, to call someone! The misfit on the right was able to dial a phone. Although he may have been just faking me out! Anyway He?, said to her? no one answers!

I couldn't believe what she said to the other.

She? said ... well, they are right behind that wall, and she actually pointed to the back wall! Seconds later a guy, person, being, strutted up beside them at the counter. It was wearing an orange vest! I obviously thought he was a parking lot attendant, {the orange vest was a give-away} or one who is in charge of gathering up the shopping carts in the lot! A job that holds one hellova lot of responsibility!

I didn't pay for a ticket to this performance. So, I asked, very seriously, if they worked here! I really wanted to know! The one sporting the orange vest, did a really good finally. He puffed up and said. "Yes! That is why we {and he pointed both thumbs at himself} are on this side of the counter, and you! he pointed two fingers, one on each hand, at me! are on that side of the counter!"

Well now, he is, definitely, either a very important employee in the company, or a complete jackass! You can make your own decision! Either way; I had about had enough of this kinda bullshit! there was a waste basket by the back wall, the wall that hides mysterious creatures like this dude.

I motioned for the a-hole to backup a foot, or two. He did. I threw that friggin' phone, as hard as I could toward the basket. I was, at one time, considered to be a champion dart shooter. Before I continue I should explain I didn't shoot at darts, I shot darts at a target!

Anyway. I hit that waste basket at approaching the speed of sound, and as I walked away, I glanced back at the mood squad, the basket was still spinning. I doubt if I am allowed in Wally's World again. I think I'll plant a friend in the store to film them escorting me out of their precious store.

Before I go to the next topic I'd like to explain how I became a good shooter of darts! I had property in New Brunswick, Canada, and that is about the best place in all of the world to live. I had an occasional party at my house, overlooking Chignecto Bay, Nova Scotia, the Bay of Fundy!

There was a dart board in the house when I bought it and at on of the earliest parties I was asked to join in a game. I wasn't very good at it, which didn't please me at all! If fact I got my ass beat seven ways from Sunday!

I had a store in Laconia, New Hampshire, at that time. It was on Canal street and there was a sporting goods store just across the street. I went over and purchased the best board they had and the best set of darts!

We closed the store at five o'clock! For the next hour I practiced shooting darts. I picked a comfortable stance and never changed it. I still set my feet in the exact same way today, when I'll shoot three games with my friend Chuck Herrick today, at five o'clock!

That took place back in 1990! I practiced religiously, until I started winning a game, or two! Then my wins were often and my confidence level was that I couldn't be beat. To this day, no matter how far behind I might get, I remain relaxed and confident I can win. And a good many times I pull out another win! Back to 1990.

I went to New Brunswick every chance I got. Sometimes I drove and other times I flew! I always wanted to take the ferry, but never got that to work into my schedule!

My next trip, after buying the dart board, was great! I kicked me some Canadian ass! I even drove to Monkton finding some shooters I remembered whipping me and repeated my wins, and settled my pride!

### *Goodbye Sears, I won t miss you!*

I retired after working for Sears in 2000. I worked there as a jewelry manager for nine years. I was the only graduate Gemologist in over 500 Sears stores!

Being a graduate gemologist likely doesn't mean much to the average person.

But, to become a guild jewelry store, carrying all of the major brands, like Rolex, etc, one has to have a gemologist on staff! You might think, a store like Sears would capitalize on that! Not Sears. Especially the jewelry buyers, likely because they were ignorant as to running a jewelry department. One of my district managers was only weeks ago, the hardware district manager! Can't be much difference between diamonds and lawnmowers, I reckon!

I have a hundred stories about my experience being taught about the jewelry business by complete a-holes! But I won't. I'll confine it to just two stories!

#1, the geniuses in the Ivory Towers in Chicago decided to have tests for all employees. The tests were tailored to the individual department product lines. Mine, of course were about jewelry!

One of the question was... "Does Black Onyx occur in nature. I choose "YES" as my answer. WRONG! Because of that and a few other similar question; I flunked! So, in order for the people working for me to pass I had to tell them which questions to answer wrong, so they would pass! It finally dawned on me that I was the only flunky in the department, so I went to the store manager and complained!

I finally had to call the Gemological Institute of America and get the exact wording covering this subject, which, incidentally, I knew ... "Black Onyx is found in nature. But, unfortunately not in a quantity enough to make cutting and polishing reasonable. Therefore, the mixed rough material is crushed and dyed black before cutting!"

The store manager called Chicago and they apologized saying the person making the test wasn't knowledgeable about jewelry! "Hmmmmmmmmm!" What the hell are they doing ... making a test about a subject they are unfamiliar with?  Doesn't appear the person giving them the assignment was qualified to do that, either!

Makes one wonder how far up the ladder this goes? All the way, I suspect!

I received a phone call about a week later, from Chicago. They asked if I was interested in making the jewelry tests for them. I said, "Sure, what does the job pay?"

He said they thought I should do it as part of my job description. By now, if you have read any of my other 306 books; you know how I responded!

#2  Actually I have already forgotten what this one was supposed to be. But, luckily, I have a backup story, or 100! I've told this one before. I received a call from the assistant manager of the store, Sears in the Sarasota Square Mall. You cannot call them to verify this story, because they won't answer the phone ... cause they blew away last year! The only people I feel sorry for are the workers who weren't paid zillions like the rapist CEO's!

#3 So sue me, this was supposed to be the second one. Anyway, I have told this story before and I am going to tell it again, because I have wondered if the main person in the story ever achieved the success she so justly deserved!

I hope she left Sears and went with a company that could realize what great potential this young lady has, and sends her up the ladder taking advantage of her talents.

The story takes place in Tampa at a district jewelry meeting. I was recognized as a gemologist for the first time, out of many dozens of meetings I had attended. The company person who was going to put on the presentation was young lady of Cuban or Puerto Rican descent!

She was extremely attractive and opened her presentation by saying she was aware of my credentials and experience and hoped if she made a mistake that I would, please, correct her! I'm not one for accolades, but I mostly appreciated her being alertness and awareness! Right from the start I felt it was going to be a good meeting.

Spanish ladies tend to add motion to most every word they speak. And they are off times very well blessed with a more than adequate form.

She put on an exceptional talk and I never had to correct her. One in awhile I think she was a bit unsure of what she had just said and glanced in my direction. I would just nod in approval. She would smile and continue on.

It was approaching break time. She was standing aside an easel of a large diamond design. It illustrated all of the facets, numbered them, etc. She was now starting to feel at ease and I could see her confidence was building.

I wish I could remember her name, instead of saying she this and she that! Any way ... she finished pointing out and naming all of the facets. She then pointed to the bottom tip of the diagram saying the diamond didn't come to a point. Instead it was ground and polished and is one of the flat facets. She explained the reason for not coming to a point was that having it flat reduces the chance of it getting chipped, or damaging other diamonds in a parcel of loose diamonds.

She went on to explain that diamonds are the hardest of all gemstones, but one diamond rubbing against another would cause damage to one, or both! She was really getting into a groove as lunch break approached.

Just before breaking for lunch she explained the facet you might mistake for a point was called a culet, from the French *culus* meaning *bottom*! With that she said we could take a break and to meet back here in a half hour.

She stood by her diamond display as everyone left. I was the last to leave, intentionally, and I stopped by her and said I thought she was doing a magnificent job, and if she didn't mind my saying so, I thought she had a magnificent *Culus*!

She reacted by giving me a couple of punches with her fist, on my chest! My God, that girl was strong! We laughed and went downtown Tampa for lunch!

I am not worried about her. I am sure she is doing just fine!

************

Yes, I am starting to run down. I guess you thought I never would. One last thing ......If you want a night out full of entertainment just go to the next Haverhill Heritage Commission meeting. There is likely to be another fake election which is worth watching. It's like no one cares that they are making complete unadulterated fools of themselves.

If I didn't know better I would think it is an Edgar Bergen and Charlie McCarthy skit!

And it is all because they have bias against the people that are asking to join a commission that is about to fail, and likely should be shut down because of the actions they take, to control who does and who doesn't join their little Jim Jonestown community.

I guess that makes me Mortimer Snerd!

## The Mill Street Bridge

Before you get in a frenzy; I know the Mill Street Bridge isn't a memorable building! But if you were walking up the rail trail, under the structure, you would feel like you were walking through a building, of sorts!

This seven span timber frame trestle was constructed in 1938 to carry Mill street over the railroad line. This is the second trestle in this location, replacing a similar 1917 trestle built to separate the grade of Mill street and the railroad.

The trestle is constructed of timber-framed bents set on granite footings, with granite abutments.

The railroad line began as the White Mountain Railroad in 1853. BBy the time the trestle was constructed the line was operated by the Boston and Maine Railroad.

who embarked on a grade separation campaign during the late 1910's.

The bridge was eligible for listing in the National register under criterion "C", as the best surviving example in the state that embodies distinctive characteristics of a now-rare bridge type. The period of Significants under criterion "C" is 1938.

This bridge (trestle) has been dismantled and a new bridge is nearly completed! Flat bed trucks have arrived with huge stone blocks and the construction appears to be on schedule.

I was at the site while they were digging out for the foundation work. From high above the machinery looked like Tonka toys instead of huge earth moving equipment!

The new bridge is nearly finished, come and look for yourself!

## DDDDDat's All Folks!

You might like my newest suspense novels
featuring Jason Downer and Dee Dee!
Here are the titles if you have missed any, or decide you want to give them to friends as gifts!

#1, Sundown on Turtle Beach
*a married dudes girlfriend is missing*

#2, Venice Beach Dilemma
*Sun and Dee Dee take on a case when a man is arrested for killing his wife and her lover*

#3, Missing in Belize
*SunDee Investigations is hired to find two college girls that have become missing on vacation*

#4 The Tampa Kidnapper
*The entire crew at SunDee Investigations get involved in Belize*

#5 Belize Battalion
Another investigation in Belize, involving most of the gang!

**I am in hopes of presenting Sun, Dee Dee, and all of their cohorts in a new 13 week TV series!  Watch for it!**
**JEH    info@wmtn.biz**


**You might enjoy some of my other books......**


**Woodsville, NH Thru a Young Boy's Eyes  7981046**
**Woodsville, a Railroad Town  3653258**
**Woodsville, NH, THE Governor's Farm, and other stuff  7909960**
**What You May Not Know About Pike, NH  5120002**
**What You May Not Know About Piermont, N H  5726464**
**What You May Not Know About Our Filling Stations  5355223**
**What you may not know about Narrows and Haverhill-Bath Covered Bridge  5110103**
**What You May Not Know About Lamarre Brick Yard  5416911**
**What You May Not Know About Ira Whitcher  5484740**
**Wells River, where rivers meet  3383913**
**Haverhill New Hampshire's Fake History    #301**
**Guess What I Got!  ... OLD!    #303**


**Or, google  James E. Hobbs books**

You might like my new series of suspense novels....
*Definitely Not Bedtime Stories ...*
*and, hopefully, the next 13 week television series!*


JEH

www.ingramcontent.com/pod-product-compliance
Lightning Source LLC
Chambersburg PA
CBHW061758250726
48657CB00001B/187